Alex Smith and Veenu Jain

Cambridge IGCSE™
and O Level

Business Studies

Workbook

CAMBRIDGE
UNIVERSITY PRESS

CAMBRIDGE
UNIVERSITY PRESS

Shaftesbury Road, Cambridge CB2 8EA, United Kingdom

One Liberty Plaza, 20th Floor, New York, NY 10006, USA

477 Williamstown Road, Port Melbourne, VIC 3207, Australia

314–321, 3rd Floor, Plot 3, Splendor Forum, Jasola District Centre, New Delhi – 110025, India

103 Penang Road, #05–06/07, Visioncrest Commercial, Singapore 238467

Cambridge University Press is part of the University of Cambridge.

It furthers the University's mission by disseminating knowledge in the pursuit of education, learning and research at the highest international levels of excellence.

www.cambridge.org
Information on this title: www.cambridge.org/9781108710008

First published 2019

20 19 18 17 16 15 14 13 12 11 10 9

Printed in Dubai by Oriental Press

A catalogue record for this publication is available from the British Library

ISBN 978-1-108-71000-8 Paperback

Additional resources for this publication at www.cambridge.org/9781108710008

Contents

How to use this book

This workbook accompanies the Cambridge IGCSE™ and O Level Business Studies coursebook and aims to help you consolidate your business studies knowledge as well as develop the important skills of analysis and evaluation.

The workbook has been designed as a flexible resource to support you on your business studies skills journey. The questions are designed to provide further opportunities for you to check your understanding of particular business topics as well as your ability to provide solutions to a variety of business scenarios.

Learning summary
Each unit begins with a summary list that briefly sets out the learning aims for each section, helping you to progress through the content and understand key concepts.

Learning summary

Before completing the activities in this unit, you should review your work on the following business topics:

- **needs**, **wants**, **scarcity** and **opportunity cost**
- the importance of specialisation to businesses and consumers
- the purpose of **business activity**
- what is meant by 'added value'
- how a business adds value.

KEY TERMS

Primary sector: firms whose business activity involves the extraction of natural resources.
Secondary sector: firms that process and manufacture goods from natural resources.
Tertiary sector: firms that supply a service to consumers and other businesses.
Private sector: the part of the economy that is owned and controlled by individuals and companies for profit.
Public sector: the part of the economy that is controlled by the state or government.
Mixed economy: an economy where the resources are owned and controlled by both the private and the public sectors.

Key terms
Key terms and their definitions have been included at the start of each unit to help you identify and understand important concepts within a particular topic.

Scaffolded activities
Scaffolded activities provide an opportunity for you to apply your knowledge and develop your skills in analysis and evaluation to consolidate your learning. Activities include help notes, which will be reduced as you become more confident towards the end of your course.

Activity 1.1

This activity is designed to test your understanding of business activity.

Tyche Plc is a sports goods manufacturer that makes footwear for different types of sporting activity, such as running, football and hockey. Many of the business's customers buy their goods to play sports, but also for everyday use in their lives. Tyche has experienced a good year and has seen its sales increase by 15%.

a Identify **four needs** involved in business activity. **[4]**
Reflect on the things that people must have as they lead their everyday lives.

b Outline **two** of the **wants** involved in Tyche's business activity. **[4]**
Think about the goods that you buy but do not actually need.

c Explain **two** reasons why Tyche's sales might have increased in the last year. **[6]**
Here you need to make a link between changes in wants/needs and Tyche's sales.

TIP
'Explain' questions want you to set out the reasons why and how things happen.

Tip
Tips provide additional context and useful guidance to accompany the main text and activities.

Reflection: Consider the way that you have used the case study examples from P & M Ltd to support your answers to the question. Could you improve on the amount of context that you include in your answers?

Reflection

There are opportunities for you to reflect not only on what you have learnt, but also on how you got there. Were there things you found particularly difficult or easy? Perhaps you could have approached a particular task differently and achieved a different outcome? Reflecting regularly on your learning can help you understand how you work best and what you can do to improve that next time.

All exam-style practice questions and sample answers in this title were written by the author(s). In examinations, the way marks are awarded may be different.

Exam-style practice questions

Quick Route Ltd is a taxi business that operates as part of the tertiary sector in a local town. The business is now the biggest firm in the market with over 80 drivers. Quick Route has grown significantly over the last four years and bought out another taxi firm two years ago. Along with its regular taxi customers, Quick Route also has many contracts with local private businesses and public accounts with a hospital and the local authority. In addition, Quick Route operates a small fleet of executive cars that it uses for exclusive work at the luxury end of the market. This enables it to charge a much higher price above the normal fare.

a Define the term 'public sector'. **[2]**

b Define the term 'tertiary sector'. **[2]**

c Outline **two** reasons why Quick Route might have expanded its business. **[4]**

d Explain **two** possible ways that Quick Route's decision making is affected by being a private sector business. **[6]**

e Do you think that Quick Route's business has been helped by targeting three different types of customer? Justify your answer. **[6]**

Total available marks: 20

Exam-style case study

Boiling Point Ltd

It has been a difficult two years for Boiling Point Ltd since the Ethiopian business was launched. Boiling Point manufactures high-quality kettles which it sells within the domestic Ethiopian market and it also wants to export to Europe. The CEO, Eskor, won an enterprise award this year for his success in running Boiling Point. The award showed how well Eskor had managed the business since it came very close to failing in its first six months.

One of the business's strengths is its ability to add value to its product and this has made the business very attractive to potential investors. Boiling Point is a good employer and is highly regarded by its staff and by the local community.

Eskor is very ambitious and wants Boiling Point to grow. He is particularly keen to start a joint venture with the established producer #Kitchen Services which specialises in kettles and water heaters for the industrial market. Appendix 1 shows information on #Kitchen Services.

Eskor has approached the Ethiopian government for a grant to support Boiling Point's growth and expansion into the European market. The government is very keen to support manufacturing businesses that want to export.

Appendix 1

Information about #Kitchen Services

- It has 20 successful years in the market and is very profitable.
- It has very good links with the market for kettles and water heaters in the domestic market and in the European market.
- There have been several recent reports of unethical behaviour within the business, such as paying very low wages to its employees.

Exam-style practice questions and case studies

Exam-style practice questions will help you to understand the style and structure of questions you may encounter in an examination.

Improve the answer...

There are some ways to improve this answer. Did you think about these?

The strengths of this answer show sound understanding of the terms 'economies of scale' and 'profits'. There is detailed discussion of two of the factors but discussion of the third factor is missing.

There could also be better discussion of economies of scale by, for example, considering some of the issues associated with economies of scale, such as diseconomies of scale emerging as Boiling Point increases in size.

There needs to be an effective conclusion that considers all three benefits of growth but makes the case for one factor over the others.

Improve the answer...

'Improve the answer' sections follow exam-style practice questions and encourage you to use your own knowledge and skills to think about how a sample answer, written by the authors, could be improved.

This workbook is designed to help you develop your skills in Cambridge IGCSE™ and O Level Business Studies and to enhance your learning of the course material. A key part of this is developing your skills in the way you answer business-related questions.

Study skills

The first section goes through each aspect of what it takes to effectively demonstrate your knowledge of business studies. To do this, it goes through the following areas:

- the use of command words in questions
- how to apply your analytical and evaluative skills to business scenarios
- answering questions using business data, charts and numbers
- improving your skills through reflective learning.

How the activities are structured

Each unit in the workbook focuses on the different business studies topics followed in the coursebook. The book is structured to help you in the following ways:

Use of stimulus material

As you progress through your course, you will become familiar with answering questions in the form of short case scenarios. These questions are designed to help you practise applying key business skills to realistic business scenarios. It is important that you remember to refer to the information in the case scenarios to support your answers to questions.

Supporting guidance on activities

Many of the questions at the beginning of the workbook offer support and guidance designed to help you better understand particular question types and also build your skills. As you progress through the workbook and become more confident in answering business study questions, the amount of guidance will be reduced. Each section also includes helpful tips to improve your question technique.

Exam-style practice questions

At the end of each section you will find a series of exam-style practice questions, including short answer, data response and case study questions. The authors have written a selection of sample answers to the exam-style practice questions, with suggestions about how they could be improved. Here, you will have the opportunity to apply your own skills in order to think about and write a better answer in each case.

Importance of reflection

A key part of learning how to develop your business studies skills is through reflection. At the end of each unit, there is a guide to aspects you can reflect on based on the learning themes. When you are doing the activities, however, you should be continuously reflecting on the whole learning process and asking yourself how you can improve your answers.

Online answers

There are online answers to each activity. An effective way to improve your learning is to do the questions and use the answers to reflect on how well your business studies skills are developing.

The aim of this book is to develop and support your learning in business studies. Many of the activities put you in the position of a manager who is looking at a business and has to assess the issues and challenges that the business faces when making decisions. The questions test your knowledge and understanding of business studies but also give you the opportunity to think like a manager and make the judgements needed for effective decision making. As a company CEO once said: 'Don't guess when you are making decisions; always base your decisions on logic and reasoning.' It is worth bearing this in mind when you are answering the questions.

I would like to thank the editor of this book, Felicity Radford, for her invaluable help and advice throughout the writing process.

Alex Smith

What is expected from your answers to questions?

Throughout this book, you are going to answer questions that develop and improve your business studies skills. There are two key things to focus on:

- What makes an 'excellent answer'?
- How can you learn the skills needed to produce 'excellent answers'?

This section of the book looks at the areas that you will need to concentrate on to make your business studies skills as good as they can be.

The importance of command words in questions

The skills that you will need to demonstrate will differ, depending on the command words used in different questions. The command word is the term or phrase that appears in a question that is asking you to demonstrate a particular skill. The command words that you will become familiar with during your business studies course are:

- 'State' – to set out an idea, term or point in a few words.
  State the breakeven output of a business's new project.
- 'Calculate' – to work out a value from set facts and figures.
  Calculate the gross profit from the figures in an income statement.
- 'Define' – to give the precise meaning of a term.
  Define the term 'labour turnover'.
- 'Identify' – to name or select an idea, term or point.
  *Identify **four** elements in the process of recruitment and selection of employees.*
- 'Outline' – to set out the main points.
  *Outline **two** types of external finance that a business might source to raise additional funds.*
- 'Explain' – to establish relationships and reasons why and how things happen.
  *Explain **two** reasons why strong branding is important to a business.*
- 'Justify' – to make a reasoned argument that is supported by evidence.
  Do you think that a business should expand its market by locating in another country? Justify your answer.
- 'Consider' – evaluate the information you have been provided with.
  Consider whether you think Sani is right to relocate her business operation to Mexico.

Developing skills for business studies

There are specific areas of knowledge and skills that you will learn whilst studying business, and this workbook contains questions which will help you to develop and practise these skills, including:

- knowledge and understanding of business facts and theory
- application of business facts and theory
- analytical skills in the way you use evidence and reason
- evaluative skills by making judgements and recommendations.

You will not be expected to demonstrate all of these skills at the same time, but the different questions will develop these skills in stages as you move through a whole question.

The workbook contains exam-style practice questions at the end of each unit which have been written by the authors. You will find sample answers (also written by the authors) for you to work on improving, which will help you to practise how to further develop your skills.

Knowledge and understanding

You will need to demonstrate an accurate knowledge and understanding of all the material you have studied during your course. All types of question are designed to help check your knowledge and understanding, but knowledge-based questions often use the command words 'identify' and 'state'. Here is an example of how you might need to show your knowledge and understanding. Look at the sample answer given and decide what you might do to improve it before reading on:

Q Identify **four** types of external stakeholder that the retailer LNM might have. **[4]**

Have a go at this question and then compare your response to this sample answer. How does your answer compare?

Government, local community, customers and suppliers.

Application

To answer questions effectively, you need to apply your knowledge and understanding of business facts, ideas and theory to business situations. This means answering clearly and accurately by using the case study material. This is crucial in answering all types of questions. Here is an example of a question which uses the 'outline' command word:

Q Outline **two** types of sources of finance that ABC Farm might use to buy a new piece of equipment. **[4]**

Have a go at this question and then compare your response to this sample answer. How does your answer compare?

ABC Farm could use retained profit from previous years. This is profit made each year by the farm and the funds are accumulated in the bank to buy, for example, a new tractor. It could also lease the machinery from a finance company. ABC Farm pays a sum of money each month to a finance company to pay for a new tractor but doesn't actually own the tractor.

Analysis

Analysis is a crucial skill that you need to develop in business studies and questions where you need to demonstrate this skill often contain the command word 'explain', or 'justify'. This means making a point and then making links to how and why something happens. Consider this question, for example:

Q Explain **two** reasons why toy manufacturer XYZ has seen a fall in its employees' motivation in the last year. **[6]**

Have a go at this question and then compare your response to this sample answer. How does your answer compare?

The new manager in the factory has adopted an autocratic leadership style and changed people's working patterns to make their jobs more repetitive, which has had a bad effect on worker morale. Autocratic management can often lead to conflict between managers and workers which reduces motivation. Repetitive tasks can make work boring which does not satisfy one of Herzberg's hygiene factors and this can reduce motivation.

Evaluation

The ability to evaluate is a very important skill needed for business. Questions that use the command word 'justify' are looking for you to make judgements about the argument that you have developed in your answer. You will need to demonstrate effective knowledge and understanding, application, and analysis but you will then need to build on this by making judgements about the points that you make. This can be done by:

- stressing the relative importance of the point that you have made
- suggesting a weakness or opposing view
- considering how the argument developed could change over time
- questioning any assumptions that you have made.

This is an example of a question which requires evaluative skills:

Q Is the best way to improve labour productivity at RST car manufacturing to invest in new technology on the production line? Justify your answer. **[6]**

Have a go at this question and then compare your response to this sample answer. How does your answer compare?

Investing in new technology means that RST could buy new machinery that it could use on the production line to improve worker efficiency. If worker efficiency rises then this would lead to a rise in labour productivity. Labour productivity can be measured in output per employee (output/number of employees). This would mean that RST can produce more cars from its existing workforce and increase its revenue and profits. The problem for RST will be the cost of the machinery and it may mean that some workers will lose their jobs. Investing in new machinery may also be disruptive in the short term and RST needs to think about the effect that the new machinery might have on worker motivation. Another way to improve productivity could be to improve worker motivation by using financial incentives, but if worker productivity is limited by machinery then investment in machinery would be the best option. In conclusion, to be competitive in the market where other firms are improving productivity, it is important to invest in new technology.

Using stimulus and case study material

All the questions in this workbook are based on stimulus material. In the main sections of the book, this appears in the form of short business scenarios that provide data and additional context for a particular question. In the exam-style practice questions, you will encounter stimulus material in both the exam-style practice questions and in the exam-style case studies located at the end of each section of the book.

The stimulus material and the questions in the book are designed to help you apply the knowledge and skills you have acquired during your course.

- For short answer and data response questions, you will be provided with a piece of stimulus material which will take the form of a business scenario. It is important that you refer to these business scenarios and any supporting data in your answers.
- For case study questions, you may be presented with additional stimulus material in the form of appendices. You should remember to refer to any relevant data that may support your argument in your answers.

Using numbers and charts

Some of the questions that you answer will involve the use of data, diagrams, charts and calculations. Being able to use this type of information effectively is a very important business skill. The questions in the book that involve the use of numbers and charts will require you to:

- show knowledge and understanding of data used, for example by showing your understanding of a pie chart that shows the market share of different businesses in an industry
- be able to apply data to a business situation, for example, explaining what a rise in cash inflow means for a business's liquidity
- be able to calculate a figure from a given set of data, such as using revenue and cost to calculate profit

- analyse data to explain business issues, such as what rising revenue figures tell us about the effectiveness of a marketing strategy
- evaluate the usefulness of data and make judgements. If, for example, the gross profit figure is falling, does it mean that the business is failing to control cost efficiently or is it caused by another factor such as falling prices?

This is a sample question and answer

The table shows the income statement for food manufacturing business RST for the last two years.

$m	Year 1	Year 2
Sales	4	4.8
Cost of sales	2.2	2.9
Good profit		

Have a go at this question and then compare your response to this sample answer. How does your answer compare? How would you improve the sample answer?

a Calculate the growth profit of business RST for 2016 and 2017. **[2]**

Gross profit = sales – cost of sales

Year 1 $1.8m
Year 2 $1.9m

b Outline the difference between revenue and cost of sales. **[4]**

The revenue is the income of business RST which is calculated by multiplying units sold by selling price. Cost of sales is purchase cost of the inventories used to produce the final good sold.

c Explain **two** reasons why RST's sales revenue might have increased from 2016 to 2017. **[6]**

The first reason that RST's revenue might have increased is because of effective advertising for its food products which makes them more attractive to consumers and leads to an increase in demand. As demand increases, RST's revenue would rise. The second reason might be an increase in the price of a competitor's products which means that some of their consumers switch to RST's goods as a lower-priced alternative. This leads to a rise in RST's units sold and revenue.

d Is a rise in the gross profit for RST a sign of a high-performing business? Justify your answer. **[6]**

Gross profit is one way of measuring the performance of RST because it tells us about RST's ability to sell its food products and generate revenue. The more revenue that RST generates, the better its performance on this measure because, for example, it may be making food products that are high quality and attractive to the consumer. The second reason the rise in gross profit is an indicator of high performance at RST is because the business is able to manage its cost of sales effectively, which keeps costs low and increases gross profit. RST may be doing this by negotiating a low price with its suppliers. This rise in gross profit is, however, not compared with other firms in the market who have increased their gross profits by more than RST, which would mean its performance had not improved as much. In conclusion, rising gross profit is normally seen as an improvement in performance if it is sustained over a period of time and relative to other firms in the market.

Improve your skills through reflective learning

At the end of each unit in this book, there is a short section on reflection which gets you to think about what you have learnt in the unit and how you could improve next time. If you follow the process of reflection throughout the book, your understanding of the subject will improve and you will write better answers to questions.

Here is a reflective process you could use when you are doing the activities in this book:

- Complete one of the activities in the book.
- Review your answers and critically examine them against the assessment objectives.
- Compare your answer to the answers given online.
- Think of the areas that you need to improve.
- Put the improvements that you have thought of into practice when you do the next activity.

Consider this example of the reflective process by completing the following sample question

ARC Limited is a small retail business that owns shops that cut keys for consumers. The business was started four years ago by Luis, who is operating as a sole trader. The market is highly competitive with a number of supermarkets operating a similar service within their stores and a new online service that has affected ARC for the last two years. Luis would like to develop the business by expanding into the industrial market by selling keys and locks to businesses. This will require significant finance and an investor has already approached ARC to finance the new venture in return for being made a partner.

a State **two** sources of external finance that may be available to ARC. **[2]**

Sample answer: Bank loan, trade credit.

Reflection: How good is my knowledge on sources of finance?

b Define the term 'sole trader'. **[2]**

Sample answer: This is a business owned and controlled by one person who takes all the risks and all the profits.

Reflection: Did I use precise business terminology?

c Outline how competition for ARC might affect the demand for its products. **[4]**

Sample answer: Competition from supermarkets might affect the demand for ARC's products because they are a competitor to ARC. If customers go to the supermarket to get their keys cut and not ARC then the sales revenue of ARC will fall. The online business also represents competition. If customers use the online business, they will buy fewer keys from ARC and its revenue will fall.

Reflection: Did I apply the case example clearly to support my answer?

d Explain **two** reasons why expanding into the industrial market might benefit ARC. **[6]**

Sample answer: The industrial market means selling keys and locks to a new market. The new market would mean more revenue to ARC because it would be selling more products and industrial customers may buy keys in very large quantities.

Reflection: Am I making it clear why ARC's expansion into the industrial market will be beneficial to the company?

e Do you think Luis should accept the partnership offer of the new investor? Justify your answer. **[6]**

Sample answer: By taking finance from the investor, Luis would get the funds to invest in the new industrial market and this would give him the opportunity to grow his business. It would also enable him to spread the risk of his business across different markets in case one market went into decline. It would, however, mean that he would lose some control over the business because the investor wants to become a partner. This could be a problem if the new investor wanted to take ARC in a direction that Luis did not want. Luis should take the funds from the outside investor because the new competition from supermarkets and online businesses is going to make it increasingly difficult for ARC and the new partner's input could be useful to ARC.

Reflection: Have I developed my argument to justify the conclusion I have come to?

Section 1
Understanding business activity

1 Business activity

Learning summary

Before completing the activities in this unit, you should review your work on the following business topics:

- **needs**, **wants**, **scarcity** and **opportunity cost**
- the importance of specialisation to businesses and consumers
- the purpose of **business activity**
- what is meant by 'added value'
- how a business adds value.

KEY TERMS

Business activity: the process of producing goods and services to satisfy consumer demand.

Need: a good or service which is essential to living.

Want: a good or service which people would like, but is not essential for living.

Scarcity: there are not enough goods and services to meet the wants of the population.

Opportunity cost: the benefit that could have been gained from an alternative use of the same resource.

Consumer goods: products which are sold to the final consumer. They can be seen and touched, for example computers and food.

Consumer services: non-tangible products such as insurance services, transport.

Capital goods: physical goods, such as machinery and delivery vehicles, used by other businesses to help produce other goods and services.

Activity 1.1

This activity is designed to test your understanding of business activity.

TIP

To outline, you will need to set out the main points in your answer by describing the need and want that the sports footwear is satisfying.

Tyche Plc is a sports goods manufacturer that makes footwear for different types of sporting activity, such as running, football and hockey. Many of the business's customers buy their goods to play sports, but also for everyday use in their lives. Tyche has experienced a good year and has seen its sales increase by 15%.

a Identify **four needs** involved in business activity. **[4]**

Reflect on the things that people must have as they lead their everyday lives.

b Outline **two** of the **wants** involved in Tyche's business activity. **[4]**

Think about the goods that you buy but do not actually need.

c Explain **two** reasons why Tyche's sales might have increased in the last year. **[6]**

Here you need to make a link between changes in wants/needs and Tyche's sales.

Activity 1.2

This activity tests your knowledge of the different factors of production.

A car manufacturer uses the following resources to produce and sell its cars:

- land
- labour
- capital
- enterprise.

Identify the type of resource in each case by completing Table 1.1.

Resource	Type
The family that initially started the business	
Plastic to use in car interiors	
Workers who work on the production line	
Metal to use in the production car bodies	
Employees who work in the finance department	
Robot technology used on the production line	
The business's IT system	
The shareholder in the car manufacturer	

Table 1.1

Activity 1.3

This activity develops your understanding of scarcity and opportunity cost.

D7 Ltd is a small jewellery business that buys diamonds and makes high-quality rings, necklaces and brooches. D7 is a small family business that is struggling to raise the finance to buy increasingly expensive diamonds. As a result of spending so much money buying diamonds, the business has had to postpone buying a new diamond-cutting machine.

a State the opportunity cost of D7 Ltd spending increasing amounts of money on diamonds. **[2]**

To 'state', you need to demonstrate knowledge and understanding by setting out the opportunity cost of spending on diamonds in clear terms.

b Explain, using the concept of scarcity, why diamonds are expensive. **[6]**

Think about the limited supply of diamonds and the high demand that there is for them.

Activity 1.4

Consider the following goods and services in Table 1.2 and identify whether they are:

- consumer goods
- consumer services
- capital goods.

Product	Type of good or service
A dress bought by a mother for her daughter's birthday party	
A new building bought by a school	
A personal computer sold in an electrical retailer for home use	
Financial advice offered by a bank to a person thinking of retiring	
The ticket bought for a professional football match	
The vehicles bought by a distribution company	

Table 1.2

Activity 1.5

P&M Ltd is a national magazine company that has over 50 magazine titles that it sells throughout East Asia. It specialises in producing magazines for the sports and recreation market for consumers who are serious enthusiasts. Titles include monthly golf, cycling, fitness and walking magazines. P&M Ltd is seen as a high-value-added business. Its retail price is high but consumers are willing to pay a high price for the quality of the product.

The business is soon to open a new office in the United States to develop its magazine titles there. This will require a $15 million investment in a new building and equipment. To do this, P&M will have to give up a plan to upgrade its IT.

TIP
Use precise terminology when you are defining key terms.

a Define the term 'value added'. **[2]**

b Outline the buyers' want being satisfied by P&M magazines. **[4]**

Clearly set out why people read the type of magazines that P&M Ltd produces.

TIP
'Justify' means supporting your case with evidence or argument. This requires evaluative skills, which means making a judgement about how P&M benefits from adding value.

c State the opportunity cost of P&M Ltd opening an office in the United States. **[2]**

Try to clearly show the alternative choices that the business will have to give up due to opening the office in the US.

d Outline the capital and labour resources that P&M Ltd will need when it opens its new office in the United States. **[4]**

It is important to give examples of the labour and capital resources when it opens the new office.

e Consider whether you think that P&M Ltd is right to specialise in magazines for 'serious enthusiasts'. Justify your answer. **[6]**

Start by explaining and analysing the advantages for P&M Ltd of specialising and then explain and analyse that disadvantages of P&M Ltd specialising. Finish by evaluating the overall impact to P&M Ltd of specialising.

Reflection: Consider the way that you have used the case study examples from P&M Ltd to support your answers to the question. Could you improve on the amount of context that you include in your answers?

2 Classification of businesses

Learning summary

Before completing the activities in this unit, you should review your work on the following business topics:

- **primary**, **secondary** and **tertiary sector** business activity
- the changing importance of the classification of business activity by sector for developing and developed economies
- how business enterprises are classified in the **private sector** and the **public sector**.

KEY TERMS

Primary sector: firms whose business activity involves the extraction of natural resources.

Secondary sector: firms that process and manufacture goods from natural resources.

Tertiary sector: firms that supply a service to consumers and other businesses.

Private sector: the part of the economy that is owned and controlled by individuals and companies for profit.

Public sector: the part of the economy that is controlled by the state or government.

Mixed economy: an economy where the resources are owned and controlled by both the private and the public sectors.

Activity 2.1

This activity is designed to check your understanding of the primary, secondary and tertiary sectors of the economy.

In Table 2.1, there is a list of goods and services which need to be matched with the business activity they are associated with.

TIP
When you are choosing whether a good is primary, secondary or tertiary, think about how the good or service is produced.

Good or service	Business activity (primary, secondary, tertiary)
Dentist	
Fishing	
Musical instrument	
Fridge	
Social media app	
Soya beans	
Personal computer	
Airline ticket	
Diamond mining	

Table 2.1

Activity 2.2

This activity will help you to check your understanding of how business operates in the private and public sectors.

A local hospital in a town near Mumbai is owned and controlled by the government and is the biggest employer in the town. People work as doctors, nurses, chemists, laboratory staff and administrators. They also use the services of two limited companies. One provides cleaning services and the other does the hospital's catering.

a Outline why the hospital is in the public sector and the limited companies that provide its services are in the private sector. **[4]**

Try to focus clearly on the factors that make an organisation private or public sector.

b Explain why the hospital and the businesses that service it are an example of organisations in a **mixed economy**. [6]

This 'explain' question wants you to show your analytical skills by making connections between the ownership of an organisation and the nature of the economy.

Activity 2.3

This activity checks your knowledge and understanding of a public sector tertiary business.

Ganji Academy is a local state-funded and managed school based in Bangladesh. It is a secondary school that has 1500 students from a local town and surrounding area. The school has a good reputation for discipline and academic standards. The school's mission statement is 'Giving our students the best all-round education possible' and all management decisions taken have this mission in mind.

a State whether the Ganji Academy is in the primary, secondary or tertiary sector. **[1]**

b Explain how Ganji's decision making is affected by being a public sector rather than a private sector business. **[6]**

It is important here to think about the role of profit in influencing private and public sector businesses.

Activity 2.4

These questions get you to look at the aims and decision making of a private sector tertiary business.

The market for coffee shops has grown dramatically over the last ten years. Large chains of coffee shops are now present in many high streets along with many independent coffee outlets. Australian consumers enjoy lattes, cappuccinos and espressos as well as the high-quality pastries, cakes and sandwiches that go with them.

a State **two** possible aims of the decisions made by businesses in the coffee shop market. **[2]**

Think of all the aims that businesses might have in the private sector.

b Outline how the coffee shop market in Australia makes private sector decisions in terms of what, how and for whom to produce goods and provide services. **[4]**

A strong answer would use an example of how resources are allocated through the coffee shop market.

Activity 2.5

The aim of this activity is to test your understanding of a market where there is some debate as to whether businesses should operate in the private sector or the public sector.

NPV rail is a train company that operates trains in the southern region in Argentina and it is in the tertiary sector of the economy. It is a private sector business that aims to make a profit of $200 million each year. The company also has the aim of increasing its profit by 4% in each of the next four years. One of the ways that the company aims to increase its profit is by introducing new technology and cutting costs. Many of the workers at NPV are worried by the threat of redundancies in an attempt to reduce costs.

a Define the term 'tertiary sector'. **[2]**

Write your definition precisely using exact terminology.

b Outline **two** possible objectives of NPV rail as a private sector business. **[4]**

Think about the aims that private sector businesses have to be successful.

c Do you think that NPV as a private sector business is good for its customers and workers? Justify your answer. **[6]**

Start your answer by explaining why NPV being a private sector business is good for customers. For example, it has the freedom to provide services that satisfy consumer demand. Then evaluate this by, for example, explaining how private sector businesses may increase prices to consumers to increase their profits.

TIP

When you are answering this 'justify' question, you need to make judgements about whether shareholders and workers benefit from NPV being in the private sector.

Reflection: Think about the things that you have learnt about the different types of sectors that businesses exists in. What do you need to know in order to give clear justifications for answers in this unit?

3 Enterprise, business growth and size

Learning summary

Before completing the activities in this unit, you should review your work on the following business topics:

- **entrepreneurs** and enterprise
- **business plans**
- how to measure business size
- why some businesses grow
- why some businesses fail.

KEY TERMS

Entrepreneur: an individual who has an idea for a new business and takes the financial risk of starting up and managing it.

Business plan: a detailed written document that outlines the purpose and aims of a business and that is often used to persuade lenders or investors to finance a business proposal.

Revenue: the amount that a business earns from the sale of its products.

Start-up business: a newly formed business. Such a business usually starts small, but some might grow to become much bigger.

Activity 3.1

The aim of this activity is to improve your knowledge of the characteristics of an entrepreneur.

Costanza is going to start her own social media business. Complete Table 3.1 by matching these examples of how Costanza might show the characteristics of a social entrepreneur:

- has ideas about a new app
- knows a large number of people in the industry
- has used her house to secure a loan to start the business
- sorted out a funding problem by arranging a new type of loan
- sells her business enthusiastically
- works very long hours
- wants to achieve a **revenue** of $5m in three years
- is never afraid to stand up in front of her workforce and talk about her vision for the business
- has a degree in business and an accountancy qualification.

Think about some of the well-known entrepreneurs you know when considering the characteristics of entrepreneurs.

Characteristic	Example
Innovative	
Self-motivated and determined	
Self-confident	
Multi-skilled	
Has strong leadership qualities	
Takes initiative	
Results-driven	
Risk-taker	
Good networker	

Table 3.1

Activity 3.2

These questions help to develop your understanding of what is in a business plan and how it might be useful to different stakeholders.

Himari is close to starting a new business in Japan. After resigning from her job with a management consultancy firm, she wants to open a shop selling greetings cards. The local market for greetings cards is growing strongly and there is a clear opportunity for her to start a successful business. She has approached an important investor to raise finance and they have asked for a detailed business plan. Himari is interested in government support that might be available to new small businesses.

a Identify **four** ways that the government could support Himari's new business. **[4]**

b Outline **two** elements that might be in Himari's business plan. **[4]**

Here you need to take an element of a business plan, such as financial forecasts, and set out what might be in the forecast.

c Explain **two** reasons why Himari's business plan might be useful to the investor. **[6]**

Take something from the business plan, such as financial forecasts, and link this to information that will be useful to the investor.

Activity 3.3

This activity helps you to look at how the sizes of businesses are measured.

Home-shop PLC is a large retail organisation based in Mexico that employs 70 000 workers and has revenue of $1.2 billion. Out-there PLC is another Mexican business. It is a social media company that employs 25 000 people and has revenue of $3.8 billion. The Mexican government gave significant support to Out-there PLC when it was a small **start-up business** just 10 years ago.

a State **two** other ways that you would measure the size of a business other than revenue and number of employees. **[2]**

b Explain why it is difficult to compare the size of the retail business with the social media business. **[6]**

This 'explain' question is making you analyse by making links between the way that business size is measured in different industries. Think about, for example, the number of people needed to provide the service in a retailer compared to a media company.

TIP
For this 'state' question, you just need a list of two points here.

c Do you think that it is right for governments to support start-up businesses such as Out-there PLC? Justify your answer. **[6]**

Start your answer by explaining the benefits to the Mexican economy of government support for new start-ups such as bringing innovation into new markets. Then evaluate this by, for example, discussing the financial cost to the government of state intervention.

Activity 3.4

The aim of this question is to consider the reasons why organisations grow and to investigate the problems of growth.

TEMPO manufactures musical instruments for the Swedish market. The business was started in 1999 as a small family firm but has grown in size and is now looking to expand by selling in overseas markets. Martin, the CEO of TEMPO, has driven growth very hard since he took charge three years ago. One option for expanding into overseas markets is for TEMPO to buy a local manufacturer in Germany.

TIP

'Explain' questions are testing your analytical skills. In this question, try to reason links between the problems that you identify and their effect on TEMPO.

a State **two** ways that TEMPO could expand its business. **[2]**

b Outline **two** reasons why TEMPO might want to expand its business. **[4]**

Think about the benefits that the business might gain from growth.

c Explain **two** problems that TEMPO might face as it tries to expand its business by buying the German manufacturer. **[6]**

Try to set out the problems of growth for TEMPO, such as diseconomies of scale, and analyse the impact of these problems on TEMPO.

Activity 3.5

These questions make you think about issues facing small businesses.

Salma is planning to open her first business, which will be a small fast-food restaurant that specialises in the growing organic takeaway food market in Jordan. The food she intends to serve is all sourced from local farms, which is very popular with local people. Her emphasis will be on high quality and good value for money. Salma is an expert in cooking organic food and she wants to employ skilled, like-minded people in her business. The local fast-food market is, however, very competitive. When Salma approached the bank for a loan, they said she was in a strong position to be successful but warned her about the high risk of business failure amongst new small businesses. The bank is also concerned about her lack of business experience.

a Identify **four** reasons why businesses might fail. **[4]**

Remember that you just need to make a list of reasons here.

b Outline **two** benefits to Salma's fast-food restaurant of being a small business. **[4]**

Think about the fast-food restaurants that you know and why they might benefit from being small.

c Do you think that Salma is in a good position to start a successful business? Justify your answer. **[6]**

Begin your answer by explaining the strengths that Salma's business might have to make it successful, such as her expertise as a cook. Then evaluate this by considering some challenges that Salma might face, such as her lack of business experience.

Reflection: Consider the things that you have learnt about how and why businesses grow. How can you use examples more effectively in your answers to illustrate the issues associated with business growth?

4 Types of business organisation

Learning summary

Before completing the activities in this unit, you should review your work on the following business topics:

- the characteristics of different types of business organisations in the private sector
- differences between **unincorporated businesses** and limited companies
- risk, ownership and **limited liability**
- business organisations in the public sector.

KEY TERMS

Unincorporated business: a business that does not have a legal identity separate from its owners. The owners have **unlimited liability** for business debts.

Unlimited liability: if an unincorporated business fails, then the owners might have to use their personal wealth to finance any business debts.

Limited liability: the shareholders in a limited liability company which fails only risk losing the amount they have invested in the company and not any of their personal wealth.

Private limited company: often a small to medium-sized company; owned by shareholders who have limited liability. The company cannot sell its shares to the general public.

Public limited company: often a large company; owned by shareholders who have limited liability. The company can sell its shares to the general public.

Ordinary shareholders: the owners of a limited company.

Activity 4.1

This activity assesses your understanding of the risk, ownership and liability associated with a sole trader and a partnership.

Five years ago, Sam Magoge started off as a sole trader offering his services as a plumber. His business has grown substantially and he has built himself a very good reputation, known for good-quality service and completing jobs on time.

He wants to expand and also start taking up painting and decorating jobs. To keep up with the demand, he needs someone to work with him permanently. He is evaluating two options, either to become a partnership or to continue on his own and hire more employees instead.

a Define the term 'partnership'. **[2]**

Make sure that you include the number of people involved and identify at least one more feature.

b State the difference between limited and unlimited liability. **[2]**

Focus on debt and the risk associated with the business.

c Identify **two** differences between a sole trader and a partnership. **[4]**

d State **two** reasons why a sole trader might find it hard to compete with larger firms in the same industry. **[4]**

This question requires you to analyse the characteristics of a sole trader.

e Do you think that Sam should engage a partner or carry on working as a sole trader and hire more employees instead? Justify your answer. **[6]**

Identify one or two important advantages and disadvantages for Sam of forming a partnership and develop at least one.

Identify one or two important advantages and disadvantages for Sam of being a sole trader and develop at least one.

Compare the two. Assess the advantages/disadvantages of each and evaluate which might be best suited in this case.

TIP

When comparing and choosing between two options, always analyse the advantages and disadvantages of each. This will help in justifying your choice.

Activity 4.2

In this activity, you will have to use your knowledge and understanding of private and public limited companies.

TM Textiles Pvt. Ltd has been manufacturing towels and bed linen for ten years now. It is currently owned by a very close group of ten friends and family members and communication is very fast. The company has been very successful and has established itself as a trusted local brand. It wants to expand its operations further and wants to sell its products to the international market. It needs to buy new machinery and expand its current site. The directors of the company want to go public but some of the **ordinary shareholders** are reluctant to turn from a **private limited company** to a **public limited company**.

a Define a limited company. **[2]**

Explain what is meant by a limited company.

b Outline **two** reasons why some of the shareholders are reluctant to become a public limited company. **[6]**

Identify the features of a public limited company and analyse why they might be disadvantages.

Remember to answer the question in context.

c Explain **two** differences between private and public limited companies. **[4]**

The question is not specific to the business scenario so focus on analysing the differences rather than answering in context.

d Do you think that TM Textiles Pvt. Ltd should go public or take a loan from a bank to finance its expansion? Justify your answer. **[6]**

Consider and analyse both the advantages and the disadvantages of the two methods in context; going public versus remaining private and taking a loan.

Evaluate and justify your recommendation.

Activity 4.3

In this activity, you will be relying on your understanding of the characteristics of a franchise.

Nanda has been working as a hotel manager for ten years now but feels that it is time to move on and set up something on his own, such as a restaurant. While he thinks that he has good experience and expertise in the hospitality industry, he is not fully confident about starting up on his own and does not want to start an unincorporated business. With the money that he has saved in the last ten years, he has decided to buy a franchise in a popular national fast-food chain.

a Define a franchise. **[2]**

Keep your explanation clear and concise. An example will not help in a definition question.

b Explain why Nanda does not want to start an unincorporated business. **[4]**

This question is very specific to Nanda so explain the answers in context, using the information from the question.

c Identify **two** factors that affect the type of organisation that a person chooses to start their own business. **[4]**

The question is not specific to the business scenario so focus on analysing the factors rather than answering in context.

d Explain **four** advantages to Nanda of owning a franchise. **[8]**

Identify four advantages and then analyse them in context.

Reflection: What do you need to consider when applying your knowledge to a business scenario?

objectives

Learning summary

Before completing the activities in this unit, you should review your work on the following business topics:

- need for business **objectives**
- different business objectives
- objectives of social enterprises
- internal and external stakeholders
- objectives of **stakeholder** groups.

KEY TERMS

Objective: a statement of a specific target to be achieved. Objectives should be SMART.

Stakeholder: an individual or group which has an interest in a business because they are affected by its activities and decisions.

Activity 5.1

This activity checks your understanding of the need for different types of business objectives.

Swami and Vina are both software developers, and have been partners for three years, making websites for small- to medium-sized businesses. They have developed a large client base and are finding it hard to cope with the increasing demand for their services. They have realised that they need to expand their business.

They have some friends who are experts in the same field and have helped them in the past. Swami and Vina are forming a private limited company and have asked their friends to join them. They have named their new company TekSmart Pvt. Ltd and are thinking about what business objectives to set for their company.

a Define a business objective. **[2]**

This is a simple question which only requires a definition.

b Identify **four** out of the five criteria that should be used to set clear and effective objectives. **[4]**

c Explain **two** objectives that the owners of TekSmart Pvt. Ltd could set and how they are relevant to the business. **[6]**

Use your knowledge on this topic to identify possible objectives and explain them as relevant to the business.

Activity 5.2

This activity assesses your understanding of the objectives of a social enterprise.

Kamaria owns a small shop in Zambia, selling handicraft items. Kamaria likes to source her items personally from the villages close by. When doing this, she has noticed the great talent that the people have and also their lack of knowledge about how to sell their products.

Looking at the challenges faced by the people in the villages, Kamaria started a social enterprise to support them. It provides the necessary funding and space for the local people to create handicraft items and receive a salary.

Kamaria has got in touch with a few public corporations who can help grow the small handicraft industry in the area by giving the villagers some basic training in running and managing a small business and holding exhibitions for them to show their products.

a Define a social enterprise. **[2]**

b Explain how the objectives of Kamaria's social enterprise are different from that of her shop. **[4]**

Remember to apply your explanation to the business.

c Identify **two** characteristics of a public corporation. **[2]**

d Explain **two** ways that the public corporations might be able to help the village people who make the handicrafts. **[4]**

Read the question carefully to identify how the public corporations might help and explain the benefit of their assistance.

Activity 5.3

This activity assesses your understanding of the different types of stakeholders and how their objectives differ.

CHL Group Pvt. Ltd, a family owned business, is a producer of luxury chocolates. It has a factory in its home country and buys its main ingredient, cocoa, from another country. It has a hardworking workforce and a good relationship with its suppliers. For two years, CHL Group's main objective has been survival, but now it wants to expand and has profits and growth as its main objectives.

Local pressure groups have been demanding that CHL Group stops using its suppliers from another country as they are known to use unethical practices. Also, the pressure groups want CHL Group to use the locally grown cocoa as it will be good for the local suppliers and the home country's economy. The shareholders of the company are not so sure about changing suppliers as they feel that the local cocoa is not of the same quality.

a Outline the **two** main types of stakeholders and give an example of each. **[4]**

This is another 'outline' question. Make sure that your examples use the context from the scenario.

b Identify **three** stakeholders of CHL Group and explain their objectives. **[6]**

Think of both internal and external stakeholders and explain their objectives in the context of this business scenario.

c Consider why the objectives of CHL Group have changed from survival to profits and growth. **[4]**

Think about the different considerations that a business needs to think about when it starts and then once it has established itself.

d Identify **two** stakeholders who may have conflicting objectives. **[4]**

Think about the demands of the pressure groups and the impact that these would have on different stakeholders.

TIP

Though stakeholders are all affected by business decisions, they all have different objectives.

Reflection: What do you need to consider when analysing a business decision?

All exam-style practice questions and sample answers in this title were written by the author(s). In examinations, the way marks are awarded may be different.

Exam-style practice questions

Quick Route Ltd is a taxi business that operates as part of the tertiary sector in a local town. The business is now the biggest firm in the market with over 80 drivers. Quick Route has grown significantly over the last four years and bought out another taxi firm two years ago. Along with its regular taxi customers, Quick Route also has many contracts with local private businesses and public accounts with a hospital and the local authority. In addition, Quick Route operates a small fleet of executive cars that it uses for exclusive work at the luxury end of the market. This enables it to charge a much higher price above the normal fare.

a Define the term 'public sector'. **[2]**

b Define the term 'tertiary sector'. **[2]**

c Outline **two** reasons why Quick Route might have expanded its business. **[4]**

d Explain **two** possible ways that Quick Route's decision making is affected by being a private sector business. **[6]**

e Do you think that Quick Route's business has been helped by targeting three different types of customer? Justify your answer. **[6]**

Total available marks: 20

Exam-style case study

Boiling Point Ltd

It has been a difficult two years for Boiling Point Ltd since the Ethiopian business was launched. Boiling Point manufactures high-quality kettles which it sells within the domestic Ethiopian market and it also wants to export to Europe. The CEO, Eskor, won an enterprise award this year for his success in running Boiling Point. The award showed how well Eskor had managed the business since it came very close to failing in its first six months.

One of the business's strengths is its ability to add value to its product and this has made the business very attractive to potential investors. Boiling Point is a good employer and is highly regarded by its staff and by the local community.

Eskor is very ambitious and wants Boiling Point to grow. He is particularly keen to start a joint venture with the established producer #Kitchen Services which specialises in kettles and water heaters for the industrial market. Appendix 1 shows information on #Kitchen Services.

Eskor has approached the Ethiopian government for a grant to support Boiling Point's growth and expansion into the European market. The government is very keen to support manufacturing businesses that want to export.

Appendix 1

Information about #Kitchen Services

- It has 20 successful years in the market and is very profitable.
- It has very good links with the market for kettles and water heaters in the domestic market and in the European market.
- There have been several recent reports of unethical behaviour within the business, such as paying very low wages to its employees.

1 a Explain **two** ways that Boiling Point could add value to its kettles.

Way 1:
Explanation:

Way 2:
Explanation:

[8]

b Explain why the following **three** factors have been important to Eskor as an entrepreneur:

- innovation
- self-motivation and determination
- strong leadership qualities.

Which factor do you think is **most** important? Justify your answer.

Innovation:
Self-motivation and determination:
Strong leadership qualities:
Conclusion:

[12]

2 a Explain **two** reasons why the government might want to support Boiling Point as a growing business.

Reason 1:
Explanation:

Reason 2:
Explanation:

[8]

b Explain the following **three** benefits that Boiling Point might gain from increasing in size:

- economies of scale
- greater power to control the market
- increase in profits.

Which do you think is the **most** important benefit? Justify your answer.

Economies of scale:
Greater power to control the market:
Increase in profits:
Conclusion:

[12]

3 a Explain **four** reasons why businesses might fail.

Reason 1:
Explanation:

Reason 2:
Explanation:

Reason 3:
Explanation:

Reason 4:
Explanation:

[8]

b Consider the information in Appendix 1 about a possible joint venture between Boiling Point and #Kitchen Services and choose whether:

- Boiling Point should enter the new market on its own
- Boiling Point should enter the new market as a joint venture with #Kitchen Services
- Boiling Point should not enter the market.

Which option should Boiling Point choose? Justify your answer.

Boiling Point should enter the new market on its own:
Boiling Point should enter the new market as a joint venture with #Kitchen Services:
Boiling Point should not enter the market:
Conclusion:

[12]

4 a Explain why **four** different stakeholders would be interested in Boiling Point.

Stakeholder 1:
Explanation:

Stakeholder 2:
Explanation:

Stakeholder 3:
Explanation:

Stakeholder 4:
Explanation:

[8]

b Explain the benefits of Boiling Point expanding into the European market in terms of:

- sales
- profit
- risk.

[12]

Total available marks: 80

Answering exam-style practice question e

Here is a sample answer to exam-style practice question e. The answer contains some common weaknesses. Read each part and think about how the answer could be improved.

Quick Route has been helped by having the ordinary taxi business, the account business and the luxury business because they give it the chance to target more customers [App]. The luxury market has customers who have higher incomes. These customers will pay more money for the taxi service so Quick Route will make higher profit margins on these customers [An]. The accounts customers provide regular income to the business because the work is business based and is necessary [An]. Also, if one part of Quick Route's business has a problem, then other parts of the business could help out.

Improve the answer...

There are some ways to improve this answer. Did you think about these?

This answer is quite good because it focuses on the importance of Quick Route targeting two types of customer. The reasoning for targeting the luxury market is quite well set out and discussed but the benefits of having account customers could be more fully explained. Also, the answer fails to talk about the regular customers of the taxi business, which will be the core part of its sales. The weakness in this answer is that it does not really justify the argument being made. This justification could be, for example, that targeting three groups of consumers is the best way to grow the business.

Answering exam-style case study question 2b

Here is a sample answer to exam-style case study question 2b. The answer contains some common weaknesses. Read each part and consider how the answer could be improved.

Economies of scale: Economies of scale are the cost advantages that Boiling Point would benefit from as it increases in size [K].

As a larger business, Boiling Point could negotiate lower costs for the components it buys for its kettles [App]. This would mean that its average costs would fall and it would be able to reduce its prices and increase its profit margins [An].

Increase in profits: Through its growth, Boiling Point will be able to increase its profits because it will sell more kettles and this means that it will have higher revenue [App]. Assuming that its costs rise by less than the increase in revenues, its profits will rise [Ev]. The increase in profits will give Boiling Point funds to reinvest in the growth of the business [An]. However, focusing on profits may conflict with ethical objectives if workers are not paid higher wages [Ev].

Improve the answer...

There are some ways to improve this answer. Did you think about these?

The strengths of this answer show sound understanding of the terms 'economies of scale' and 'profits'. There is detailed discussion of two of the factors but discussion of the third factor is missing.

There could also be better discussion of economies of scale by, for example, considering some of the issues associated with economies of scale, such as diseconomies of scale emerging as Boiling Point increases in size.

There needs to be an effective conclusion that considers all three benefits of growth but makes the case for one factor over the others.

Section 2
People in business

6 Motivating employees

Learning summary

Before completing the activities in this unit, you should review your work on the following business topics:

- why people work
- the meaning and importance of the workplace
- key motivational theories
- financial and non-financial methods of motivation.

KEY TERMS

Motivation: the factors that influence the behaviour of employees towards achieving set business goals.

Labour turnover: the rate at which employees leave a business.

Labour productivity: a measure of the efficiency of employees by calculating the output per employee.

Hygiene factors: the factors that must be present in the workplace to prevent job dissatisfaction.

Motivators: the factors that influence a person to increase their efforts.

Quality circles: groups of employees who meet regularly to discuss work-related problems.

Job enrichment: organising work so that employees are encouraged to use their full abilities.

Activity 6.1

This activity provides a chance to demonstrate your knowledge of why people work.

Table 6.1 contains quotes from employees in a hotel business about the things that are important to them at work. Match the following reasons listed with the quotes given:

- pay
- fringe benefits
- promotion
- training
- status
- responsibility
- interesting work
- friendship.

Quote	Reason
'I enjoy meeting so many new people working on reception'	
'I like the feeling of being in charge of a large group of employees'	
'It is really good to be able to stay at other hotels in our chain at discounted rates'	
'The income I earn as the conference manager gives me a good standard of living'	
'I like the opportunity to make progress to more senior jobs in the hotel'	
'I really enjoy the company of the team of people I work with in the kitchen'	
'I have learnt so many new skills since I've worked with this business'	
'Being the manager of the hotel means that people really look up to you'	

Table 6.1

Activity 6.2

The aim of this activity is to look at the link between employee motivation and productivity, absenteeism and labour turnover.

Roxy plc is a large food-processing business that has production plants all over the world. One of its factories has rates of **labour productivity**, absenteeism and labour turnover that make it one of the best performing food-processing producers in the country. The factory's CEO, Minh, says that the key to the business's success is the way that the employees are managed so effectively.

TIP

'Outline' questions want you to set out the main points that a question focuses on.

a Outline the difference between production and productivity. **[4]**

This 'outline' question wants you to set out the main points on the difference between production and productivity.

b Consider why well-motivated workers will have lower levels of absenteeism. Justify your answer. **[6]**

There is often a link between how satisfied people are at work and absenteeism.

c Explain **two** benefits to Roxy of more motivated workers reducing labour turnover. **[6]**

In your explanation, try to analyse the link between motivation and labour turnover by considering how motivation makes people leave or stay in an organisation.

Activity 6.3

This activity gets you to look at the application of Maslow's hierarchy of needs.

Bloom florists is a small chain of regional flower shops. The business has some problems with motivation amongst its staff. Table 6.2 sets out quotes from its employees. Match each quote in the table with the different levels in Maslow's hierarchy of needs:

- physical
- safety
- social
- esteem
- self-actualisation.

Quote	Need
'I feel under-valued because my job title is not respected'	
'The pay we get is not enough to meet the cost of living'	
'I often work on my own in the shop, which makes it boring'	
'I often worry about losing my job because people are often sacked'	
'I don't feel I can reach my potential with this business'	

Table 6.2

Activity 6.4

In this activity, you have to apply Herzberg's two-factor theory and Taylor's scientific management to an organisation.

Capture Ltd manufactures photocopiers in Italy. It employs 40 workers on the production line who have to achieve set production targets. This puts the employees under high pressure but the business does pay some of the highest salaries in the industry. Capture has appointed a new CEO who wants to change the culture of the business by moving away from the 'scientific management theory' to Herzberg's 'two-factor theory'.

a Identify **two** factors associated with the 'scientific management theory' that Capture currently uses. **[2]**

b Outline **two hygiene factors** that Capture might use if it changes to the 'two-factor theory'. **[4]**

This question is to get you to think about and set out the main points of hygiene factors such as pay and conditions.

c Explain how the use of Herzberg's **motivators** 'responsibility' and 'achievement' might raise the motivation of Capture's employees. **[6]**

Make the link between 'motivators' such as responsibility and how these might make people more motivated at Capture.

TIP

'Explain' questions want you to set out the reasons why and how things happen.

Activity 6.5

This activity helps you to develop your knowledge and application of financial rewards.

Table 6.3 contains a list of different types of financial rewards. Match each of these rewards to the example given.

Financial rewards:

- hourly wage rate
- salary
- piece rate
- commission
- bonus scheme
- fringe benefit
- profit sharing.

Example	Financial reward
The managers at an insurance company will be paid an additional $5000 on top of their salary if they achieve their performance target.	
The sales staff at a car show room are paid $500 for each car they sell.	
A retail chain pays a $4000 bonus to each of its employees because of the profit it has made.	
A shoe manufacturer pays its employees $2.50 for each pair of shoes they produce.	
Managers in public sector hospitals are paid $80 000 per year.	
The staff in a fast-food restaurant are paid $10 per hour.	
Senior staff at a publishing company are given private health insurance.	

Table 6.3

Activity 6.6

The aim of this activity is to consider how non-financial methods can be used to increase motivation.

Tarit has just taken over as a store manager of a poorly performing store that is part of a major supermarket chain based in India. One of the key problems that he has identified is demotivated staff in the store. Tarit set up **quality circles** as part of a strategy to raise staff motivation, giving employees some say in the way that he wanted to change the store and more responsibility in the decision-making process. He put a programme of changes in working systems to the quality circles which included job rotation, job enlargement and **job enrichment**.

a Outline **two** characteristics of quality circles. **[4]**

Focus on how quality circles work and their objectives.

b Explain how offering staff at the supermarket more responsibility might improve their motivation. **[6]**

Be analytical here by making the link between giving employees responsibility at the supermarket and their motivation. You could refer to Herzberg's theory here.

c Why might job enrichment improve the performance of the supermarket? Justify your answer. **[6]**

Set out the way that job enrichment might raise motivation amongst the supermarket's employees and then link this to performance by, for example, looking at how more motivated employees could be more productive.

Reflection: Think about what you have learnt about what motivates people at work. Are you more confident in analysing the way that employee motivation affects business performance? If not, what would you like to improve?

7 Organisation and management

Learning summary

Before completing the activities in this unit, you should review your work on the following business topics:

- simple organisation charts
- the role of management
- leadership styles
- **trade unions**.

KEY TERMS

Functional department: the main activities of business – finance, marketing, operations, human resources and research and development.

Hierarchy: the number of levels in an organisational structure.

Subordinate: an employee who is below another employee in the organisation's hierarchy.

Autocratic leadership: a leadership style where the leader makes all the decisions.

Democratic leadership: a leadership style where employees take part in decision making.

Trade union: an organisation of employees aimed at improving pay and working conditions and providing other services such as legal advice for members.

Activity 7.1

This activity checks your knowledge and understanding of how different types of workers fit into a business's hierarchy when it is organised by function.

Table 7.1 sets out different jobs in an organisation. Complete the table by stating which **functional department** the job is in. The activities are:

- finance
- marketing
- operations
- human resources
- research and development.

Job type	Functional department
Production line workers	
Management accountant	
Technicians involved in testing new products	
The employees that manage workers' contracts	
The team of staff that work on promotional campaigns	

Table 7.1

Activity 7.2

The aim of this activity is get you to focus on the span of control and the factors that affect it.

Hot Crust bakery operates in a large city in South Africa and in the surrounding region. It is a medium-sized family business that has seen the number of layers in its **hierarchy** increase over time as the business has grown. The new CEO Karabo wants to reduce the layers in the hierarchy. This has implications for managers who will see their span of control increase.

TIP

'State' questions ask you to express your answer simply, in clear terms.

a Define the term 'span of control'. **[2]**

b State **two** factors that might determine the span of control of a manager. **[2]**

As this is a 'state' question, simply list two factors that determine the span of control.

c Explain why the span of control tends to widen as Hot Crust reduces the layers in its hierarchy. **[6]**

Analyse the link between the number of **subordinates** responsible to a manager and the layers in Hot Crust's hierarchy.

Activity 7.3

This activity is about the way that leadership styles affect an organisation.

Pug Gym is a chain of gyms managed by Wen and Jackson, who are brother and sister. Wen is the CEO and Jackson is the financial director. They have contrasting management styles. Wen likes to make all the significant decisions and rarely delegates. Jackson is much more consultative and likes to involve the people in his team in decision making. Wen's and Jackson's contrasting leadership styles are seen as a weakness and a major investor would like Pug Gym to adopt a more democratic approach.

a Outline the ways that a manager might delegate a decision at Pug Gym. **[4]**

Focus on how a manager at Pug Gym might involve their subordinates in decision making.

b Outline **two** characteristics of the **autocratic leadership** style of management. **[4]**

Try to give examples of how autocratic managers manage their subordinates and make decisions.

c Consider why Pug Gym might benefit from a more democratic style of management through the organisation. Justify your answer. **[6]**

Start by considering the benefits of **democratic leadership** such as workers responding well to being involved in decision making, then consider the problems of democratic leadership.

Activity 7.4

In this activity, you need to show your knowledge of the different functions of management.

The following are the functions of management:

- planning
- organising
- commanding
- coordinating
- controlling.

Match the examples of the work of managers with each of the functions in Table 7.2.

Make sure that you are clear on the meanings of the individual words used to describe managerial functions as it will help you understand what each type of manager does.

Example	Function
A team of employees have to report their monthly sales figures to a manager.	
A manager holds a team meeting because they feel that the team is under-performing.	
Managers hold a meeting to work out a strategy to achieve the coming year's profit target.	
A manager puts together the resources that each team will need when they are going out to sell to customers.	
The sales manager works with the production manager to make sure that enough of the final product will be available to meet customer demand.	

Table 7.2

Activity 7.5

This activity encourages you to show your knowledge and understanding of democratic management along with the relationship between management and trade unions.

The board of directors at Asprilla Engineering Ltd are struggling with poor industrial relations between the company's management and the workforce. Several industrial disputes have been costly in terms of the firm's loss of output and their reputation amongst customers. The directors have created a strategy that will decentralise decision making, allow more democratic leadership and provide better relationships with the trade union that represents many of its workers.

a State **two** functions of company directors. **[2]**

b Outline **two** characteristics of democratic management. **[4]**

Think about the ways that democratic managers treat their subordinates and make decisions.

c Explain **one** problem associated with decentralised decision making. **[6]**

An example of what you might consider here is how increasing involvement of the workforce in decision making might affect the decision-making process.

d Why might a better relationship between Asprilla Engineering's management and the trade union benefit the company? Justify your answer. **[6]**

First analyse how the effects of better relationships between Asprilla's management and the union, such as reduced industrial disputes, will benefit the business. You could go on to discuss some of the problems of working with a trade union.

TIP

Be analytical with 'explain' questions by making links between the nature of decentralised decision making and problems caused by it.

Reflection: Consider what you have learnt about the way that different organisations are organised and managed. How effectively have you used the work of the different management theorists in your answers to the questions?

8 Recruitment, selection and training of employees

Learning summary

Before completing the activities in this unit, you should review your work on the following business topics:

- recruiting and selecting employees
- the importance of training
- methods of training
- reasons for reducing the size of the workforce
- legal controls over employment.

KEY TERMS

Internal recruitment: filling a vacant post with someone already employed in the business.

External recruitment: filling a vacant post with somebody not already employed in the business.

Job description: a list of the key points about a job, job title, key duties, responsibilities and accountability.

On-the-job training: training in the workplace, watching or following an experienced employee.

Off-the-job training: training that takes place away from the workplace, for example at college, university or a specialist training provider's premises.

Redundancy: termination of employment by the employer because the job is redundant (doesn't exist anymore) due to a restructure of the business.

Activity 8.1

The aim of this question is to check your knowledge and understanding of recruitment.

Recruiting the highest-quality staff has always been a key aim of Peace of Mind Security Ltd. The business produces security systems and is based in Dubai. It recruits employees who are well qualified and highly skilled. It rewards the people it employs with pay well above the industry average and with generous benefits. Peace of Mind Security always considers **internal recruitment** first when it is recruiting for a new position but uses **external recruitment** if there is not the appropriate person internally.

a State the difference between internal and external recruitment. **[2]**

Think about the processes of recruiting staff from inside and outside the organisation.

b Outline **two** benefits to Peace of Mind Security of using internal recruitment. **[4]**

Consider things such as recruiting employees who have good knowledge of the organisation.

c Explain why external recruitment has higher costs than internal recruitment. **[6]**

Try to make links between things such as advertising for employees and how this might increase costs.

TIP

This 'explain' question is looking for you to analyse by saying how and why external recruitment costs more than internal recruitment.

Activity 8.2

This activity will help you to apply your knowledge of the recruitment process.

Table 8.1 sets out nine stages in the recruitment process. You need to put the stages into order from 1–9, 1 being the start of the process.

Stage	Number order
A shortlist is selected from all the applicants.	
Application forms and job details are sent out.	
A person specification is produced.	
The business identifies the need for a new employee and carries out a job analysis.	
The right candidate is selected.	
A **job description** is produced.	
The job is advertised.	
Completed applications are received.	
Shortlisted candidates are interviewed.	

Table 8.1

Activity 8.3

This activity gets you to think about the strengths and weaknesses of on-the-job training.

Steam Ltd is a coffee shop chain that wants to improve the efficiency of its staff in all aspects of their work. This involves stocking and presentation in the store, making coffee, and customer service. The HR director sees training as critical to improving the efficiency of staff. She is particularly keen on **on-the-job training** in the coffee shop stores.

a Outline the difference between on-the-job and **off-the-job training**. **[4]**

b Explain **two** advantages of Steam using on-the-job training. **[6]**

Focus on the benefits of the staff in a coffee shop doing their training in the coffee shop where they will do their work.

c Explain **two** reasons why on-the-job training might not be effective for Steam. **[6]**

Think about the limitations of trying to train staff within the coffee shop, such as the implication for customers when they are being served by someone being trained.

Activity 8.4

This activity gets you to think about the impact that contract law and employment regulation have on organisations.

Jouer Et Apprendre, the French toy retailer, is suffering falling sales due to online competition and competition from supermarkets. It has decided to close 30 of its worst-performing stores to make it more competitive in the market. This is a difficult situation for Jouer Et Apprendre because of the contract of employment its workers have and laws on **redundancy**. The company is also struggling with the additional costs it has incurred due to an increase in minimum wage, along with additional health and safety regulations.

a Identify **four** details that might appear in a contract of employment. **[4]**

TIP

For 'identify' questions, write a list of specific terms.

b Outline **two** factors that Jouer Et Apprendre might take into account when deciding to retain a worker or make a worker redundant. **[4]**

Think about factors such as alternative work that the employee could do if they were kept on by the business.

c Explain how an increase in the minimum wage and additional health and safety regulations might have an impact on Jouer Et Apprendre's costs. **[6]**

Consider, for example, how a higher minimum wage might affect the wage cost of Jouer Et Apprendre.

d Consider why too much employment regulation might be bad for an employer such as Jouer Et Apprendre. Justify your answer. **[6]**

Start this answer by reasoning how employment regulation might be a problem for Jouer Et Apprendre by, for example, increasing bureaucracy. Then go on to discuss some of the benefits of regulation for business costs.

Activity 8.5

Far and Wide is a tourism business that specialises in holidays for people who enjoy outward-bound and outdoor leisure activities. It runs breaks that involve sailing, rock climbing and trekking. The company relies on specialist staff who have to be very well trained in running the holidays but also in selling the business. Training and recruitment are very important to Far and Wide and keeping their employees is also in seen as crucial. The current economic recession is proving difficult because sales have fallen and the business may need to make redundancies.

a Define the term 'job description'. **[2]**

b Identify **four** stages in the recruitment process for employees. **[4]**

c Outline how Far and Wide might use off-the-job training with its employees. **[4]**

Give an example of off-the-job training such as training at a local college.

d Explain **two** benefits to Far and Wide of using off-the-job training. **[6]**

Remember to make the link between the type of off-the-job training and how Far and Wide might benefit, such as employees being able to train without the distraction of their work.

e Why might it be better for Far and Wide to retain employees in the current economic downturn? Justify your answer. **[6]**

Try to consider the benefits to Far and Wide of keeping its employees first of all and then think about the problems of retaining them, such as wage costs when revenues are falling.

Reflection: Consider what you have learnt about the recruitment, selection and training of employees. Are you more confident in applying your skills to questions about recruitment and training? What would you like to continue to work on?

9 Internal and external communication

Learning summary

Before completing the activities in this unit, you should review your work on the following business topics:

- **effective communication** and why it is important to business
- different communication methods
- barriers to effective communication.

KEY TERMS

Effective communication: information passed between two or more people or groups, with feedback to confirm that the message has been received and understood.

Two-way communication: the receiver is allowed to respond to the message and the sender listens to the response.

Communication media: the methods used to communicate a message.

Feedback: the receiver's response to a message.

Activity 9.1

This activity will help you check your knowledge of internal and external communication.

Table 9.1 sets out the types of communication used by the tyre manufacturer A Tread Plc. Complete the table by identifying whether the method of communication is internal or external.

Example	Internal/external
An email is sent by senior managers to A Tread Plc's employees about new data protection rules.	
A Tread Plc does a telephone survey with potential customers.	
A Tread Plc's finance director has a face-to-face meeting with the bank.	
The CEO has a monthly online meeting with A Tread Plc's management.	
A Tread Plc holds a meeting with local residents who live near one of its factories.	
A monthly newsletter is posted on A Tread Plc's intranet platform for all its employees.	

Table 9.1

Activity 9.2

The activity gets you to think about effective communication.

JLK Ltd is a medium-sized advertising agency. The firm's CEO, Anastasia, sees effective communication as key to the business's success. She says: 'We are a communication business so we have to communicate effectively with all our stakeholders.' Anastasia sees face-to-face communication as critical within the organisation and strongly believes that employees should 'go and see someone if they are in the same building'.

a Outline **two** characteristics of effective communication. **[4]**

Consider how information passes efficiently between two groups or individuals.

b Identify **four** types of **communication media**. **[4]**

You just need a list of precise terms here.

c Outline **two** benefits of effective communication. **[4]**

Remember the importance of **feedback** in effective communication.

d Explain **one** reason why face-to-face communication might improve the performance of JLK. **[6]**

Try to link a benefit of face-to-face communication, such as quick feedback, to improved performance at JLK.

TIP

This 'explain' question wants you to set out the reasons why and how face-to-face communication might improve performance at JLK.

Activity 9.3

This activity tests your knowledge of communication methods.

A business uses the following forms of communication:

- oral
- written
- electronic
- visual.

Table 9.2 sets out one benefit and one limitation of these forms of communication. Match each form of communication to its benefit and limitation.

Benefit	Limitation	Communication method
personal contact between sender and receiver	no permanent record	
provides a permanent record	feedback is slower	
can be sent to many receivers at the same time	can accessed by people who are not intended receivers	
creates interest and grabs attention	can be misinterpreted	

Table 9.2

Activity 9.4

In this business scenario, you need to think about the strengths and weaknesses of electronic communication.

Open Sky Plc runs international airports in Australia. The managers at the airport use a variety of different communication methods with their employees. Open Sky has developed an app that is used by all employees and this is updated continuously with information for workers. The managers also use email as a significant source of communication. There is, however, some concern amongst staff about the amount of electronic communication Open Sky uses.

a Identify **four** types of electronic communication. **[4]**

b Outline **two** factors that might account for Open Sky's choice of electronic communication as the best method of communication. **[4]**

Think about two strengths of electronic communication as they relate to Open Sky, such as the speed of transmission and response.

c Explain **two** problems of Open Sky's use of electronic communication. **[6]**

Analyse two problems of electronic communication by making the link between, for example, the very high volume of emails a person might receive and how this might affect Open Sky's efficiency.

Activity 9.5

The aim of this activity is to make you look at the problems of and solutions to poor communication.

A local government office is having significant operational problems due to poor communication throughout the organisation. A review of the office's communication saw significant problems in terms of the channels used, a lack of trust between senders, poor **two-way communication** and overly long communication channels.

a Define the term 'two-way communication'. **[2]**

b Outline **two** reasons why long communication channels might lead to poor communication. **[4]**

Think about the possible nature of a long communication channel in a government office and the impact, for example, of having lots of people communicating in the channel.

c Explain **two** negative consequences of poor communication at the local government office. **[6]**

Try to make the link between communication getting misinterpreted and how this, for example, could affect decision making in the government office.

d Is the best way to improve communication at the local government office to insist on two-way communication and make sure that the communication channel is as short as possible? Justify your answer. **[6]**

Start by looking at the benefits of two-way and short-channel communication, such as good levels of feedback, and then evaluate these by looking at how they might affect the speed of decision making.

Activity 9.6

This activity helps you to practise answering questions on the different aspects of communication within organisations.

K&C Ltd is a small manufacturing company that wants to improve communication throughout the organisation. K&C is a family business based in Chad and it relies a great deal on traditional forms of communication such as letters and notice boards. The management are concerned about the lack of two-way communication and feedback. Because K&C is a relatively small business, managers are constantly talking to subordinates and using oral communication. The management of K&C think that they can improve communication by introducing an intranet system and an app.

a Define the term 'feedback'. **[2]**

b Outline **two** forms of written communication that the managers of K&C could use. **[4]**

Use an example, such as the minutes of a meeting, and say what would be included.

c Explain **two** benefits to K&C of using effective communication. **[6]**

Try to analyse the link between effective communication and a benefit such as reduced risk of mistakes.

TIP

Make sure that you use the case study organisation as much as you can to illustrate your answer to the questions.

d Explain **two** problems for K&C of using oral communication. **[6]**

Think about an oral communication situation and link it to a problem such as lack of a record of the communication.

e Do you think that K&C is right to introduce an intranet and an app to improve communication? Justify your answer. **[6]**

Begin your answer by setting out how the intranet and app might improve communication at K&C and how K&C might benefit from this. Then go on to consider the weaknesses of this method of communication and come to a conclusion.

Reflection: Do you feel that your confidence is improving at distinguishing between different types of questions and the best way to write answers for them? If not, how can you help yourself to improve?

Exam-style practice questions

All exam-style practice questions and sample answers in this title were written by the author(s). In examinations, the way marks are awarded may be different.

ARB is a commercial bank that operates throughout a country. It employs 25 000 people in 980 branches. ARB is struggling with internal and external communication difficulties and needs to improve its communication systems. The organisation is looking to improve electronic communication both inside the organisation and outside. ARB also has motivation problems with its employees, who feel that their relationship with management is poor, partly because of poor communication. The other management change that ARB wants to make to improve motivation is to use a more democratic management style.

a Define the term 'effective communication'. **[2]**

b State how you would measure labour productivity. **[2]**

c Outline **two** characteristics of democratic management. **[4]**

d Explain how using **two** of Herzberg's 'motivators' might improve motivation at ARB. **[6]**

e Why do you think that poor internal communication is ARB's biggest problem? Justify your answer. **[6]**

Total available marks: 20

Exam-style case study

Aspire Ltd

Aspire Ltd has been developing and marketing computer games for the last nine years. The Brazilian-based company has been successful and is now one of the leading computer games businesses in the country. The business has achieved a 20% market share and profits increased by 15% last year.

Much of Aspire's success is attributed to the way that it manages its people. It has a workforce of 55, many of whom are computer graduates and are highly skilled. Aspire's employees are well paid, earning salaries well above the industry average. The workforce feel recognised for their achievements at work and really enjoy the day-to-day tasks associated with designing computer games.

Throughout the organisation, there is a huge amount of respect for Aspire's CEO, Francesca. She is a democratic leader who believes in getting all employees involved in decision making through quality circles. Aspire is a flat organisation and managers have a wide span of control. Francesca believes that the best way to deal with highly skilled workers is to give them responsibility and to involve them in the future direction of the organisation.

Training is seen as very important at Aspire. The business believes very strongly in doing its own on-the-job training where new workers learn from existing workers, who are some of the most highly skilled people in the industry.

As an IT business, the main focus of communication is electronic. However, this is seen as a relative weakness of Aspire. Francesca wants to see more face-to-face meetings and less emailing when important decisions are being made.

1 a Explain **two** possible reasons why a well-trained labour force is important to Aspire.

Reason 1:

Explanation:

Reason 2:

Explanation:

[8]

b Explain why the following **three** factors are benefits of on-the-job training:

- It is relatively low cost.
- Employees learn the way that Aspire wants.
- Employees are producing while training.

Which benefit is the **most** important? Justify your answer.

Low cost:

Learn the way that Aspire wants:

Producing while training:

Conclusion:

[12]

2 a Explain **two** benefits to Aspire Ltd of a highly motivated labour force.

Benefit 1:

Explanation:

Benefit 2:

Explanation:

[8]

b Explain how the following factors might motivate workers at Aspire:

- salary and wage
- recognition of achievement
- the quality of the work itself.

Which do you think is **most** important in motivating employees at Aspire? Justify your answer.

Salary and wage:

Recognition of achievement:

The quality of the work:

Conclusion:

[12]

3 a Explain **four** factors that influence the span of control at Aspire.

Factor 1:

Explanation:

Factor 2:

Explanation:

Factor 3:

Explanation:

Factor 4:

Explanation:

[8]

b Explain how the following **three** factors affect the leadership style of Aspire's CEO, Francesca:

- the nature of the workforce
- the personality of the manager
- the task to be completed.

Which do you think is the **most** important factor affecting Aspire's CEO? Justify your answer.

Nature of the workforce:

Personality of the manager:

Task to be completed:

Conclusion:

[12]

4 a Explain **four** benefits to Aspire of effective communication.

Benefit 1:

Explanation:

Benefit 2:

Explanation:

Benefit 3:

Explanation:

Benefit 4:

Explanation:

[8]

b Aspire wants to move away from electronic communication to oral communication. Explain an advantage and a disadvantage of each of these methods of communication. Which do you think is **most** effective? Justify your answer.

Electronic communication

Advantage:

Disadvantage

Oral communication

Advantage:

Disadvantage

Conclusion:

[12]

Total available marks: 80

Answering exam-style practice question d

Here is a sample answer to exam-style practice question d. The answer contains some common weaknesses. Read each part and consider how the answer could be improved.

The first motivator is improving the work itself and making the work enjoyable [K]. At ARB this could mean giving an employee lots of different banking tasks so that they don't get bored. If workers at the bank enjoy their work, they will be more motivated [App].

The second motivator is recognition. This means recognising a worker's achievements at work [K]. This could mean making sure that workers get a bonus if they perform well at work. This may mean acknowledgement of achieving targets set in a worker's appraisal [App].

Improve the answer...

There are some ways to improve this answer. Did you think about these?

This answer considers two relevant 'motivators' and they are reasonably well explained. The first motivator is the work itself; it needs to be interesting and varied. This answer could be improved by being more specific about how to make jobs more interesting, such as by giving the workers at ARB a variety of different tasks which constantly change. The next part of the answer is recognition at work and the 'bonus' example is a relevant one.

Answering exam-style case study question 1b

Here is a sample answer to the exam-style case study question 1b. The answer contains some common weaknesses. Read each part and consider how the answer could be improved.

Low cost: On-the-job training is low cost because outside trainers or college places don't have to be paid for by Aspire [K] [App].

Learn the way that Aspire wants: By doing its own training, Aspire will be able to teach its employees the skills it wants to, which is very important in a skills business such as computer game design. [An]

Producing while training: The employee who trains on-site will be able to work while they are training, which adds to Aspire's output, although workers training new employees may not be as productive [Ev].

Conclusion: The most important factor is probably employees being able to train the way that Aspire wants. Aspire is a leading business so its methods are successful and these can be passed on to new employees [Ev]. This may, however, add to the time and work of existing employees but developing the Aspire method is probably worth it [Ev].

Improve the answer...

There are some ways to improve this answer. Did you think about these?

This answer covers all three benefits correctly, but the benefits could be developed more fully in certain places. While the reduced cost of training in-house is recognised, there could be some mention of the cost of existing staff doing the in-house training in terms of lost output.

The point about Aspire training people the way that it wants is well made but this could be further discussed by considering the new ideas that may have been missed out on if employees had gone to an outside trainer.

The point about on-the-job training giving employees time to work as well as train is a valid one and this is evaluated by saying how workers being trained may not be as productive.

The conclusion is a good one because it focuses on the most important benefit of on-the-job training – that employees are trained the way that Aspire wants – and justifies this by focusing on the expertise of current Aspire employees to do the training effectively.

Section 3
Marketing

10 Marketing, competition and the customer

Learning summary

Before completing the activities in this unit, you should review your work on the following business topics:

- the role of marketing
- why markets change and how businesses respond
- **niche marketing** and **mass marketing**
- **market segmentation.**

KEY TERMS

Customer base: the group of customers that a business sells its products to.

Niche marketing: developing products for a small segment of the market.

Mass marketing: selling the same product to the whole market.

Market segment: a part of the whole market in which consumers have specific characteristics.

Market segmentation: dividing the whole market into segments by consumer characteristics and then targeting different products to each segment.

Activity 10.1

The aim of this question is to help you understand how the market affects business.

RinxTV is a cable television platform. It is a major provider in a number of countries where it operates news, sports, film and entertainment channels. The business has grown significantly over the last five years by developing the sports that it shows, particularly football. RinxTV has also invested significantly in the major drama productions that it shows. The business's CEO, Andre, sees effective marketing as a way of further growing the business and consolidating RinxTV's **customer base**.

a Outline the difference between customer base and **market segment**. **[4]**

Think about this in the context of the market for cable television.

b Consider how RinxTV might identify consumer wants in its market. **[4]**

Consider how businesses research the market to find out about consumers.

c Explain how RinxTV might use sports and drama shows to build customer loyalty. **[6]**

The key to this question is how a television business gets people to keep watching its programmes over a period of time.

TIP

When you are answering questions on the external environment, think about the products that you buy and how they are affected by different factors in the market.

Activity 10.2

This question provides an opportunity for you to practise applying your knowledge of factors affecting consumer demand.

In Table 10.1, match the reason why the sales of a product might change and the examples given from different markets.

Reason	Example
The price of the product	A house builder experiences a rise in demand because average wages in the economy have increased in the last two years.
The price of competitors' products	The market share of a sports goods company rises significantly when a business pays for its tennis racket to be used by the world's number one tennis player.
Changes in consumer income	A low-cost airline loses sales because of the fall in price of a major international airline.
Changes in tastes and fashion	The sales of a novelty toy rise by 200% in a year because it is seen as a 'must have' product by children.
Spending on advertising and promotion	A drugs company sees a rise in demand for a drug used to treat arthritis suffered by people over a certain age.
Changes in population size and structure	A newspaper business decides to aggressively discount its product.

Table 10.1

Activity 10.3

These questions help to develop your understanding of the impact of the external environment on marketing.

Punto Libro Books Ltd is a publishing company that produces and sells books. The company was founded over 100 years ago and is now one of the largest publishing companies in the country. The last few years, however, have seen challenging conditions for Punto Libro Books Ltd. The major change has been the growth in online books and the move towards digital books. The government also increased the minimum wage and introduced new health and safety regulations which have increased the costs of the business. There has also been increased competition from overseas publishers as free trade has increased.

a Identify **four** different government actions that might affect Punto Libro Books Ltd. **[4]**

b Outline how an increase in the minimum wage and new health and safety regulations might increase Punto Libro Books Ltd's costs. **[4]**

Try to say how regulations and wages might increase costs, such as how a rise in the minimum wage might increase Punto Libro Books Ltd's labour cost. An example would be really useful here.

c Explain why an increase in the digital market for books has been a problem for Punto Libro Books Ltd. **[6]**

You need to make the link between the competition that digital books represent to physically published books and how this might affect the sales of Punto Libro Books Ltd.

Activity 10.4

In this activity, you need to think about niche marketing and mass marketing.

Cleanall PLC is a major multinational company that produces household consumer goods. One of its bestselling product lines is toothpaste. Cleanall PLC's lead brand is called Total Clean and it has the biggest market share in the toothpaste market. Cleanall PLC has just bought a company that specialises in toothpaste made from the highest-quality materials and it sells for three times the price of Cleanall. This is a niche market product that is targeted at high-income consumers.

a Outline the difference between niche marketing and mass marketing. **[4]**

b Outline **two** benefits to Cleanall PLC of selling the expensive brand of toothpaste in a niche market. **[4]**

Consider, for example, how Cleanall PLC can achieve a higher price for its product by selling to high-income consumers.

c Explain how Cleanall PLC can increase its profits by selling its brand Total Clean to a mass market. **[6]**

One link you can make here is, for example, by explaining how selling to a mass market can lead to economies of scale and how this might increase profit.

Activity 10.5

In this activity, you need to consider the strengths and weaknesses of market segmentation.

TIP

'Justify' means making a reasoned argument that is supported by evidence on how market segmentation may help Yousport Ltd achieve its objectives.

Yousport Ltd is a major sports goods manufacturer. As part of its strategic planning for the next five years, it is looking to increase its market share in the sports goods market by targeting three market segments: women, young athletes and runners. To grow its market in these areas, it is working on new product designs and promotional methods.

a Define the term 'market segment'. **[2]**

b Identify **two** types of market segmentation that Yousport Ltd is targeting in its strategic plan. **[4]**

c Do you think that Yousport Ltd will be more successful in achieving its strategic objectives in the next five years by segmenting its market? Justify your answer. **[6]**

Begin by thinking about the benefits of market segmentation, such as designing goods to precisely meet the needs of the consumer. Then consider some of the problems of segmentation.

Reflection: This unit is designed to develop your understanding of the different ways that businesses can look at their market. Consider what you have learnt about the different ways that businesses plan and react to different parts of their markets. Which areas do you most need to focus on and improve?

11 Market research

Learning summary

Before completing the activities in this unit, you should review your work on the following business topics:

- the role of **market research**
- methods of market research
- how market research results are presented and used.

KEY TERMS

Market research: the process of collecting, recording and analysing data about the customers, competitors and market for a product.

Market orientated: products are developed based on consumer demand as identified by market research.

Product orientated: the firm decides what to produce and then tries to find buyers for the product.

Primary research: the collection of first-hand data for the specific needs of the firm.

Secondary research: the collection of data from second-hand sources.

Quantitative research: the collection of numerical data that can be analysed using statistical techniques.

Qualitative research: the collection of information about consumers' buying behaviour and their opinions about products.

Activity 11.1

The aim of this is to get you to think about how an organisation uses market research to become more market orientated.

SouthernB is a business under pressure. It is a bus company that operates in the southern region of a country. It has been heavily criticised in the media because of poor customer service. A new management team has been appointed to try to improve SouthernB's customer service and image. The key to the start of this process is effective market research. The team want to see the business become more market orientated and develop its unique selling points: comfort and reliability.

a Define the term 'market research'. **[2]**

b Identify **four** ways that market research can help SouthernB. **[4]**

c Explain how SouthernB could make itself a more market-orientated business. **[6]**

A key thing to emphasise here is how SouthernB needs to become more focused on the customer by, for example, providing extra services that give the customer a better experience.

TIP

To 'identify', you just need to give a list of the four types of market research.

Activity 11.2

In this activity, you need to show your knowledge of the difference between primary research and secondary research.

Table 11.1 sets out examples of different types of market research conducted by a cycle shop. Complete the table by identifying whether the types of research are primary or secondary research.

Example	Types of research
The marketing manager at the shop buys a market research report on the cycling market in the country.	
A person is interviewed about the types of cycling they do.	
A student who works part-time at the shop spends a week researching news articles on the internet about the cycling market.	
The shop manager sends an email questionnaire to customers asking them about their satisfaction with the shop's product range.	
The owner of the shop uses government publications to find out about population and income in the local area.	
Customers are invited to the shop for a group discussion about cycling equipment.	

Table 11.1

Activity 11.3

This activity gets you to focus on the application of primary research.

LJK Ltd is a soft drinks manufacturer that wants to find out more about its market. There has been a steady drop in the sales of its full-sugar drinks and it wants to change its position in the market to become a producer that does not produce any full-sugar drinks and concentrates on non-sugar, healthy alternatives. The management at LJK see this as a response to changes in consumer taste and as a market orientated approach. A key part of this change in strategy by LJK has been extensive primary research supported by secondary research.

TIP
This 'explain' question wants you to make links between primary research and the benefits for LJK.

a Outline the difference between a business being market orientated or **product orientated**. **[4]**

Think about the focus of the business when it is marketing its product.

b State **two** types of secondary research that LJK might have used. **[4]**

Think about a type of research such as use of government publications and how this might be used by LJK.

c Explain **two** benefits to LJK of using primary research to research the soft drinks market. **[6]**

Here you need to focus on, for example, how primary research might help get information that is precisely related to LJK's move to non-sugar drinks.

Activity 11.4

The aim of this activity is to help you consider the display of market research data and sampling.

Safe-sure Ltd produces security systems for the domestic home market. It focuses on different types of alarm systems and security cameras. The business believes that effective primary research is crucial to finding out about its customers and seeing changes in the market. Safe-sure Ltd uses sophisticated research methods involving sampling and extensive **quantitative research**. Presenting this data effectively is seen as particularly important.

a Identify **four** different ways that market research data can be displayed. **[4]**

b Outline **two** reasons why Safe-sure would use sampling as part of its market research. **[4]**

Think about the problems of trying to research the entire market.

c Why is primary market research the best way to find out the views of Safe-sure's customers? Justify your answer. **[6]**

Start by considering the benefits of primary research, such as getting information precisely related to what information the business wants. Then evaluate this by considering some of the problems of primary research such as its cost.

Activity 11.5

In this activity, you can practise applying your skills in interpreting and analysing data from charts.

The marketing consultancy Awe Ltd advises businesses on marketing strategy. To help businesses with their online strategy, it has conducted market research on the online buying patterns amongst a sample group of ten consumers. Awe recorded the number of online purchases that each member of the sample group made from 2015 to 2017. The results of its survey are shown in Figures 11.1 and 11.2.

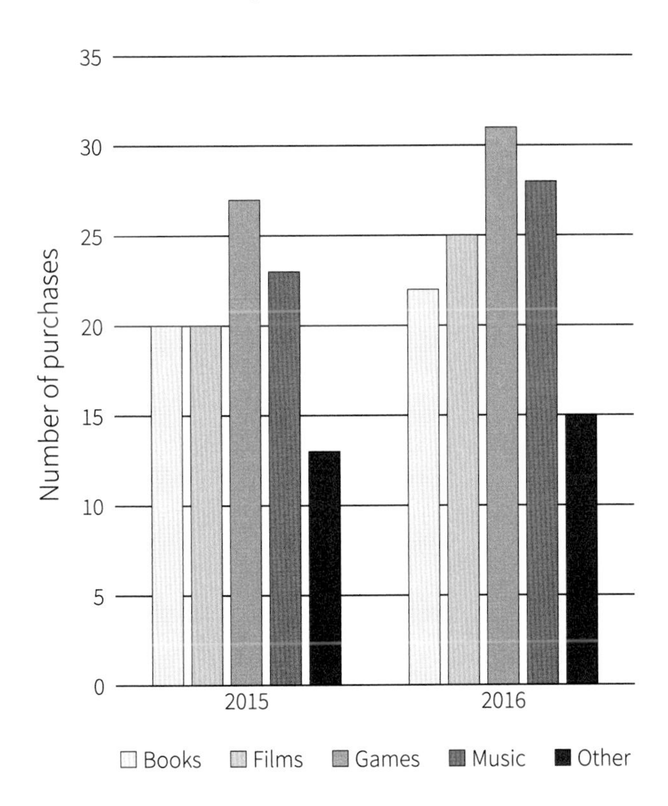

Figure 11.1

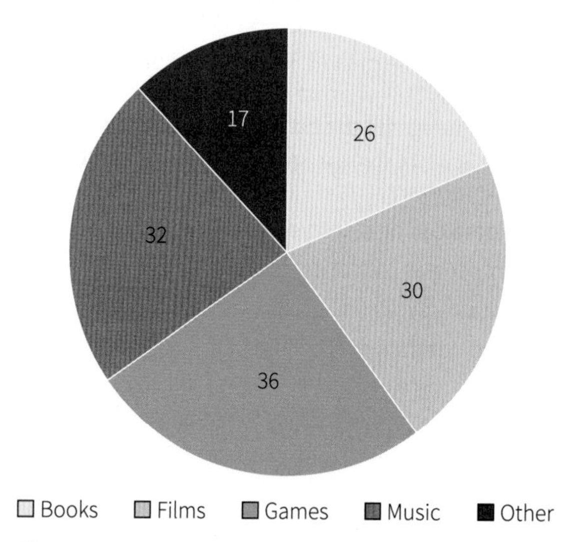

Figure 11.2

a Calculate the percentage of music purchases made in 2017 out of the total online purchases made in 2017 by the sample group. **[2]**

b Calculate the percentage increase in film purchases from 2015 to 2017 by the sample group. **[2]**

Remember to show your working.

c Do you think that the data shows a growth in value of the online sales market from 2015 to 2017? Justify your answer. **[6]**

Be specific and refer to the scenario for details about what was researched. Think about what the data can tell you and think about its limitations.

Reflection: Now that you are at the end of this unit, consider your understanding of how market research is used by organisations to improve the way that they market their products. What areas do you need to improve your understanding of?

Learning summary

Before completing the activities in this unit, you should review your work on the following business topics:

- the term '**marketing mix**'
- the costs and benefits of developing new **products**
- the role of packaging
- the **product life cycle**
- pricing methods
- price elasticity of **demand**.

KEY TERMS

Marketing mix: four marketing decisions needed for the effective marketing of a product.

Product: the goods and services produced to satisfy a customer need or want.

Brand: a name, image or symbol that distinguishes a product from competitors' products.

Product life cycle: the pattern of sales of a product from introduction to its withdrawal from the market.

Cost-plus pricing: setting price by adding a fixed amount to the cost of making or buying the product.

Demand: the quantity of goods and services that consumers are willing and able to buy.

Revenue: the amount earned by a business from the sale of its products.

Activity 12.1

This question is designed to help you check your understanding of new product development.

R&C manufactures high-quality headphones. Its leading **brand** is an 'on-ear' product with a retail price of over $300. The headphone market is competitive and R&C is always looking to develop new products. R&C is going to introduce a new 'wireless in-ear' product in response to the introduction of similar 'in-ear' products by other firms in the market. Introducing this new product has been expensive for R&C and it will need to charge a high price to cover these costs.

a State the difference between a product and a brand. **[2]**

b Outline **two** product development costs that R&C might experience when it launches its new 'wireless in-ear' product. **[4]**

Think about investment in new capital, for example, R&C might need to produce the new headphones.

c Explain **two** benefits to R&C of introducing its new 'wireless in-ear' product. **[6]**

Make the connection between the introduction of the new product and how this might increase sales **revenue** at R&C.

TIP
Remember to clearly show understanding and application in outlining the difference between a product and a brand.

Activity 12.2

This activity helps you to apply the theory of the product life cycle.

Thirm Ltd is a medium-sized food manufacturing business that specialises in high-quality soups and sauces. The business was founded in 1965 and has successfully managed sustainable growth in sales and profits. The management at Thirm has been particularly good at managing the life cycle of its products by always having new products to replace declining products and by having products in the maturity phase that can finance new product development. Thirm's marketing department is also good at using extension strategies to maintain the lives of products.

a Identify the **four** phases of the product life cycle. **[4]**

b Outline **two** characteristics of the maturity phase of the product life cycle. **[4]**

Try to set out what happens to sales and profits when Thirm is in the mature phase of the product life cycle.

c Explain **two** extension strategies that Thirm might use to extend the life of one of its brands. **[6]**

It is important to develop an example of an extension strategy, such as redesigning the product, and explain how this can maintain sales.

Activity 12.3

This activity tests your knowledge of different pricing methods.

Table 12.1 sets out the characteristics of different pricing methods.

Match the following pricing methods to their characteristics:

- market skimming
- penetration pricing
- competitive pricing
- promotional pricing
- **cost-plus pricing**.

Example	Pricing method
A confectionery manufacturer sets a discount price when it launches a new chocolate bar.	
A coffee shop bases the price of a cup of coffee on the cost of producing the coffee.	
A computer game company sets a high price when a product is first launched.	
A petrol retailer tries to match the price of other petrol retailers in the area.	
A computer retailer discounts the price of its laptops and PCs to sell more accessories.	

Table 12.1

Activity 12.4

These questions test your knowledge and understanding of different pricing methods.

YooU Air is a low-cost airline that operates all over Europe. Pricing is a critical part of its marketing strategy. If it wants to maximise its sales and profits, it needs to attract consumers with creative pricing methods. It is particularly good at attracting consumers with low fares and then selling additional services such as insurance, hotel rooms, fast-track boarding and seat selection. The finance director has a crucial role to play in pricing by insisting that the marketing department is aware that prices need to reflect costs.

a Identify **four** factors that YooU Air might consider when choosing a pricing method. **[4]**

b Outline how YooU Air could use cost-plus pricing when setting the price of a flight. **[4]**

Set out how YooU Air uses costs such as buying of the aircraft and fuel as a basis for setting a price.

c Explain how YooU Air uses loss leadership when pricing its flights. **[6]**

It is important to make the link between selling flight tickets and the other services that YooU might sell.

Activity 12.5

This activity gets you to think about how price elasticity of demand can be used by a business in its pricing decisions.

The marketing department at Pearce Hotel Group is working very hard to try to increase its revenues by pricing rooms at different rates depending on the time of week and year. The marketing director, Ashwan, is particularly keen to increase rates at weekends and during national holidays when demand means that price is not elastic. During the week, the demand for hotel rooms becomes more price elastic and he suggests cutting prices then.

a Define the term 'price elasticity of demand'. **[2]**

Give a short, precise meaning for the term.

b Outline the reason why demand for the hotel may be less elastic at weekends. **[4]**

Think about the way that consumer demand changes at different times of the week based on the peak times when people want to use a hotel.

c Explain why cutting the price of rooms during the week might increase sales revenue. **[6]**

This question wants you to make the link between pricing decisions, price elasticity of demand and revenues.

d Why is it important to base pricing decisions on consumer demand? Justify your answer. **[6]**

Consider how consumers decide where to spend their money. Evaluate this by considering other pricing factors such as cost.

TIP
This 'justify' question asks you to discuss the importance of demand in pricing decisions relative to other pricing factors.

Reflection: What skills are important for analysing and evaluating business issues to do with product and price? How confident are you about using them?

Learning summary

Before completing the activities in this unit, you should review your work on the following business topics:

- distribution channels (place)
- aims and forms of promotion
- the marketing budget
- technology and the marketing mix.

KEY TERMS

Wholesaler: a business that buys products in bulk from producers and then sells them to retailers.

Retailer: shops and other outlets that sell goods and services to the final consumer.

Promotion: marketing activities used to communicate with customers and potential customers to inform and persuade them to buy a business's products.

Advertising: paid-for communication with consumers which uses printed and visual media. The aim is to inform and persuade consumers to buy a product.

Below-the-line promotion: promotion that is not paid-for communication but uses incentives to encourage consumers to buy.

Sales promotion: incentives used to encourage short-term increases in sales or repeat purchases.

Activity 13.1

This activity helps you to think about the different distribution channels that businesses use.

Clear Wash PLC is a manufacturer of dishwasher products such as cleaning tablets, salt and rinse aid. It is a medium-sized company that has to compete with big multinationals that operate in this market. Distribution channels are crucial to Clear Wash. The majority of the business's products are sold to the customers through major **retailers**. The business also distributes through **wholesalers** who sell Clear Wash's products to small retailers. The business sells its products directly to industrial customers such as restaurants.

TIP
Make sure that you use precise terminology when you are defining a channel of distribution.

a Define the term 'channel of distribution'. **[2]**

b Outline the channels of distribution that Clear Wash's products would go through when customers buy their products from small retailers. **[4]**

Think about the different ways that a business can get its products to the customer and the intermediaries that the product will need to go through.

c Explain **two** benefits to Clear Wash of distributing some of its products through wholesalers. **[6]**

Consider the benefits that wholesalers bring by buying goods in large quantities and selling those goods in smaller quantities to small businesses.

Activity 13.2

This activity checks your knowledge of promotional methods.

Table 13.1 sets out examples of different methods of **promotion**.

Match each example with the following methods:

- **advertising**
- **sales promotion**
- personal selling
- direct mail
- sponsorship.

Example	Method of promotion
A credit card company sends offers to customers through the post.	
A chain of coffee shops offers a loyalty card to customers which gets them a free cup with every eight that they buy.	
A cosmetics business uses a major fashion magazine to promote its products through pictures of models in the magazine.	
A sports goods manufacturer pays a leading tennis player to use its rackets.	
A car dealership uses a team of employees to sell cars to customers.	

Table 13.1

Activity 13.3

This activity helps you to consider how different promotional methods and the marketing budget can have an impact on an organisation.

Holdall Ltd manufactures bags and suitcases. The company has a big online presence and favours selling directly to consumers without the use of retailers. It does, however, have a small number of its own stores that only sell the 'Holdall' brand. The directors are setting their marketing budget for next year and have increased total advertising spending by 20% in an attempt to grow Holdall's market share. Persuasive advertising is seen as particularly important in growing market share.

a Outline the difference between informative advertising and persuasive advertising. **[4]**

Remember to clearly express the difference between the two ways that advertising affects potential customers.

b Explain **two** advantages to Holdall of selling directly to customers. **[6]**

Make the link between sales people contacting customers and the impact on sales.

c Do you think that an increase in Holdall's marketing budget will increase its market share? Justify your answer. **[6]**

Begin this answer by explaining how the size of the marketing budget can affect sales and evaluate this by, for example, considering how other factors might affect market share.

TIP
With 'explain' questions, you need to analyse by making links between business theory and outcome.

Activity 13.4

Let-us-in Ltd is an online ticketing agency. The business sells tickets for major sporting events, concerts and theatre productions. Let-us-in's promotional budget is largely spent on online advertising and social media. The efficiency of the business's electronic ordering and payments system is seen as crucial to its commercial success. The company has come under pressure in recent months because its system has been hacked and the payment details of some of its customers have been taken.

a Define the term 'e-commerce'. **[2]**

b Identify **two** threats to Let-us-in of using e-commerce. **[4]**

Think about the threat mentioned in the case scenario as one example.

c Explain **two** ways that social media can be used by Let-us-in to increase its sales revenue. **[6]**

It would be useful to think about your own use of social media and the way that companies promote to you.

Activity 13.5

Wild Crocs is a jazz club in a major city in the US. The business has struggled over the last five years and has been loss-making this year. A new management team has been brought in by the owners to make the image of the club 'more modern'. Part of their marketing strategy is to change how Wild Crocs promotes itself. There will be much greater use of **below-the-line promotion** and greater use of social media. The club is going to invite in some well-known bands to raise the business's profile. This will be expensive but it is hoped to increase ticket sales in the long run.

a Identify **four** different methods of promotion that Wild Crocs might use. **[4]**

b Outline the difference between above-the-line and below-the-line promotion. **[4]**

Consider how advertising differs from other types of promotion.

c Explain **two** ways that the use of promotion using social media might increase Wild Crocs's sales. **[6]**

Remember how, for example, social media can target potential consumers very precisely.

d Do you think that working with 'well-known bands' is an effective method of promotion? Justify your answer. **[6]**

Start this answer by explaining how the 'well-known bands' might create effective publicity and go on to evaluate this by thinking about the financial cost of doing this.

Reflection: Consider the things that you have learnt about the way that businesses promote and distribute their products and how this is affected by the type of business you are studying. How well has your understanding of the importance of advertising and promotion improved?

14 Marketing strategy

Learning summary

Before completing the activities in this unit, you should review your work on the following business topics:

- marketing strategies
- **legal controls** on marketing strategy
- opportunities and problems entering foreign markets.

KEY TERMS

Legal controls: laws that control the activity of businesses.

Joint venture: an agreement between two or more businesses to work together on a project.

Activity 14.1

This activity is designed to check your understanding of marketing strategy.

Bright Bonnet Ltd is a car-washing business that operates a chain of car washes in the northern region of Thailand. The business is planning to expand its operations into another region. In order to do this, it needs to develop a marketing strategy. Bright Bonnet has three key objectives that it wants to achieve:

- annual revenue from each of the new outlets of $400000
- a market share of 15% after two years
- a unique selling point of: 'fast clean at the lowest price'.

The key tactics for the strategy are to have the latest cleaning equipment and well-trained staff.

a Define the term 'marketing strategy'. **[2]**

b Identify the **four** elements of the marketing mix. **[4]**

c Outline **two** benefits to Bright Bonnet Ltd of having a unique selling point. **[4]**

Think about the effect that the USP of a business has in the mind of the consumer.

d Do you think that Bright Bonnet Ltd benefits from having precise marketing objectives as part of its marketing strategy? Justify your answer. **[6]**

Start by explaining the benefits of precise marketing objectives such as giving managers clear direction and evaluate whether these outweigh the problems that they might cause.

TIP
Remember to think about marketing strategy as a plan to achieve objectives.

Activity 14.2

Here, you are asked to look at the legal controls on business.

Think Ltd is a German business that sells virtual reality headsets. The business is based in Munich, but its products are manufactured in China and Think distributes them all over Europe. Although the product is the very latest technology, there have been faults with it and a number of headsets have been returned. The business is successful and sales of its latest product increased by over 40% this year. Think is in a competitive market and faces competition from a well-known multinational which wants to try to push Think out of the market by its pricing method. The case is being considered by the competition authorities.

a Identify **four** types of legal control that might affect a business. **[4]**

b Consider how the multinational company might be unfair competition for Think. **[4]**

Consider how a large company can use low prices to affect Think's position in the market.

c Explain **two** reasons why producing the headsets in China might be a problem for Think. **[6]**

Reflect on the fact that using the Chinese manufacturer means that Think might not have as much control over the way that the headsets are produced.

TIP

'Justify' questions need you to show evaluative skills.

d Do you think that effective legal controls on businesses are always a good thing for consumers? Justify your answer. **[6]**

Try to debate the benefits of controls for consumers, such as production standards, against the problems of legal controls.

Activity 14.3

This activity helps you to check your knowledge of the problems of entering foreign markets.

Table 14.1 sets out the problems of entering foreign markets.

Match each example with the following problems:

- differences in legal controls
- differences in language
- lack of market knowledge
- economic differences
- social differences.

Example	Problem
A soft drinks manufacturer finds that its iced tea brand does not sell well because people in a country see tea as a hot drink.	
A washing powder has to change the name of its product because it does not translate well into an overseas language.	
An economic recession in an overseas market means that the sales of motorcycles are falling.	
A retailer opens branches in a country and is unaware that people in the country like to shop late in the evening, not during the day.	
A car manufacturer has to make right- and left-hand-drive cars.	

Table 14.1

Activity 14.4

The objective of this activity is for you to examine the issues that a business faces when it enters an international market.

Redoc Pens Plc is planning to export to a market in a developing country. Redoc has concentrated its sales in Europe and North America but is expanding its activities into developing markets which are seen to offer opportunities for growth. The market in the developing country is proving to be a challenge because Redoc lacks knowledge of consumer tastes in the market for pens and there are significant trade barriers that it will encounter when it tries to enter the market. Redoc has also had to change all its advertising and promotional material because of language and cultural differences. Redoc does have the opportunity to enter into a **joint venture** with a local pen manufacturer which will make entry into the market much easier.

a Define the term 'joint venture'. **[2]**

b Identify **two** benefits to Redoc Pens Plc of expanding into the market of the developing country. **[4]**

Think about, for example, the impact of entering new markets on Redoc's sales.

c Consider why a lack of knowledge of consumer taste and language differences might make it difficult for Redoc Pens Plc to enter the market of the developing country. **[6]**

Consider, for example, the impact that consumer taste and language have on advertising.

d Do you think that Redoc Pens Plc should enter into a joint venture with a local producer when it is entering the market of the developing country? Justify your answer. **[6]**

Here you need to debate the benefits of joint ventures, such as market knowledge, against the possible cost of joint ventures.

Reflection: Think about the things that you have learnt about the way that businesses plan for the future and put strategies into place to achieve their objectives. Are there any areas that you could focus on to improve your knowledge?

All exam-style practice questions and sample answers in this title were written by the author(s). In examinations, the way marks are awarded may be different.

Exam-style practice questions

Sequin Ltd is a fashion business that specialises in clothes for young women. Sequin sees its unique selling point as 'designer style at affordable prices'. The CEO, Masha, believes in the importance of market research as a key aspect of marketing strategy and she particularly sees the value in qualitative research. She likes to use focus groups of women to get their reaction to new designs. Masha is also passionate about effective promotion. She believes in the power of social media and Sequin's marketing department has a significant presence on sites such as Facebook and Instagram.

a Define the term 'qualitative research'. **[2]**

b State why focus groups are considered a method of qualitative research. **[2]**

c Explain how Sequin's unique selling point might increase its sales. **[4]**

d Explain **one** advantage and **one** disadvantage to Sequin of using social media to promote its products. **[6]**

e How important do you think market research is to the success of Sequin's marketing strategy? Justify your answer. **[6]**

Total available marks: 20

Exam-style case study

Spin-it Ltd

It has been a successful five years for Spin-it Ltd, a cycle hire business located near Malaga in Spain. The business was started by Louis and Celia as a rental business that targeted tourists on holiday in the resorts near Malaga. The market grew very strongly in the first three years but now growth seems to have stopped. Market research conducted by Spin-it is shown in Appendix 1. Spin-it used focus groups and a consumer survey to research the market.

Spin-it has used psychographic market segmentation to target its market by focusing on cycling enthusiasts. Celia thinks that this segment may be too narrow and feels that the business should develop a range of ordinary leisure bikes to rent. She believes that this is a market they have not developed but it is competitive and penetration pricing and extensive promotion will be needed by Spin-it to use this strategy of product development.

Louis is very enthusiastic about improving Spin-it's use of e-commerce. He is very keen to further develop the online booking system. The use of electronic payments has been improved by an up-grade to Spin-it's IT system and Louis wants to use an Instagram social media campaign to promote the new leisure bikes.

Appendix 1

Malaga cycle hire market research

Potential revenue in the local market has stopped at 15 000–18 000 potential renters per year.

The maximum rent that consumers are willing to pay per day is $20.

1 a Explain **four** reasons why consumer spending patterns might change in the cycle hire business.

Reason 1:

Explanation:

Reason 2:

Explanation:

Reason 3:
Explanation:

Reason 4:
Explanation:

[8]

b Consider the market research information in Appendix 1. Spin-it is considering **two** approaches to the market research information:

- look for a new market
- product development.

Which approach should Spin-it choose in response to the information? Justify your answer.

New market:

Product development:

Conclusion:

[12]

2 a Explain **four** ways that market research might help Spin-it develop its marketing strategy.

Reason 1:
Explanation:

Reason 2:
Explanation:

Reason 3:
Explanation:

Reason 4:
Explanation:

[8]

b Explain how the following methods of market research might be used by Spin-it to provide information about the consumer in the cycle renting market:

- focus groups
- test market
- consumer survey.

Which method do you think is **most** useful to Spin-it? Justify your answer.

Focus groups:

Test market:

Consumer survey:

Conclusion:

[12]

3 a Explain **two** reasons why market segmentation might be useful to Spin-it.

Reason 1:
Explanation:

Reason 2:
Explanation:

[8]

b Explain the following pricing methods that Spin-it could use for its new range of leisure bikes:

- marketing skimming
- penetration pricing
- competitive pricing.

Which factor do you think could be **most** effective in the successful marketing of the leisure bikes? Justify your answer.

Marketing skimming:
Penetration pricing:
Competitive pricing:
Conclusion:

[12]

4 a Explain **four** methods of promotion that Spin-it could use to promote its new shop.

Method 1:
Explanation:

Method 2:
Explanation:

Method 3:
Explanation:

Method 4:
Explanation:

[8]

b Explain how the following types of e-commerce might help Spin-it to market its cycle hire business:

- electronic payment
- online bike reservation
- promotion through social media.

Which type of e-commerce do you think is **most** useful to Spin-it's marketing strategy? Justify your answer.

Electronic payment:
Online bike reservation:
Promotion through social media:
Conclusion:

[12]

Total available marks: 80

Answering exam-style practice question e

Here is a sample answer to exam-style practice question e. The answer contains some common weaknesses. Read each part and consider how the answer could be improved.

Market research involves finding out about customers' views on Sequin and the market that it operates in [K]. By using focus groups, Sequin is able to generate ideas for new products and these can be used in the product development part of its marketing strategy [App]. The focus group could also give valuable information to Sequin on the price that consumers are willing to pay – which helps with the price element of Sequin's marketing strategy [An]. There are, however, some weaknesses in the use of market research. The information that Sequin has may not be accurate and it might give Sequin's management the wrong idea [Ev]. All in all, market research is very important to Sequin's success because it gives the views of its consumers.

Improve the answer...

There are some ways to improve this answer. Did you think about these?

This answer is strong on the benefits of market research for marketing strategy through the link between research used by Sequin and how this might support strategy. The answer questions the accuracy of the information but this could be developed further by, for example, saying that the sample size for a focus group may not be big enough to represent the market. The conclusion needs to be justified. It might say something like 'it is very important because it is crucial to generate customer views on new product development'.

Answering exam-style case study question 4b

Here is a sample answer to exam-style case study question 4b. The answer contains some common weaknesses. Read each part and consider how the answer could be improved.

Electronic payment: Electronic payment is a good way of making it easier for customers to pay for bike hire and for Spin-it to collect cash [App]. All businesses need to collect cash effectively to maintain their liquidity so electronic payment could help Spin-it improve its cash flow.

Online bike reservation: Online bike reservation makes it easier for customers to rent bikes from anywhere that there is an internet connection [App]. This will make sure that bikes are reserved for customers when they are on holiday, which improves Spin-it's customer services and could lead to an increase in its sales revenue [An].

Promotion through social media: The use of promotion through social media can help Spin-it target potential customers with online advertising. This form of promotion is cheap and it can be effective [An].

Conclusion: The most effective use of social media would be online advertising such as Instagram used to promote the new leisure bikes.

Improve the answer...

There are some ways to improve this answer. Did you think about these?

The first point about electronic payment starts quite well but it moves on to liquidity, which is important to Spin-it but it is not so relevant to its marketing strategy. The discussion of online bike reservations is good because it focuses on how this can improve customer service and increase revenue, which is a direct marketing benefit. The final point on social media promotion is reasonable, but it lacks depth. The answer could go on to develop, for example, how online advertising can be used to target specific customers. There is a conclusion, but it is limited because there is no real explanation of which social media type is the most useful. The answer could have discussed, for example, how social media can be targeted specifically at bike users and how it is relatively low cost compared to other advertising media.

Section 4
Operations management

15 Production of goods and services

Learning summary

Before completing the activities in this unit, you should review your work on the following business topics:

- the **production** process
- production methods and how these are influenced by technology
- the difference between goods and services
- how to explain, measure and increase **productivity**
- why businesses need to hold and control **inventories**.

KEY TERMS

Production: the process of converting inputs such as land, labour and capital into saleable goods, for example shoes and cell phones.

Productivity: a measure of the efficiency of inputs used in the production process, especially labour and capital.

Inventories: the stock of raw materials, work in progress and finished goods held by a business.

Lean production: the production of goods and services with the minimum waste of resources.

Job production: the production of items one at a time.

Batch production: the production of goods in batches. Each batch passes through one stage of production before moving on to the next stage.

Activity 15.1

In this activity, you will need to consider the nature of production and productivity in an organisation.

Dax Breit manufactures tractors that are sold all over the world. It is the market leader and has a market share of 31% in the world market. Dax Breit's best performing factory is in Indonesia where its factory has the highest level of productivity of any tractor factory in the world. The plant produces 150 000 tractors a year and has 2000 employees. The key to this factory's success is well-trained and motivated employees along with some of the latest technology on the production line.

a Outline the difference between production and productivity. **[4]**

Think about the relationship between the tractors produced and the number of employees.

b Outline the equation to calculate productivity at Dax Breit's Indonesian plant. **[4]**

c Calculate the productivity of Dax Breit's Indonesian plant. **[2]**

Clearly showing your working here.

d Explain why well-trained and motivated employees on the production line might increase productivity at Dax Breit. **[6]**

Try to make the link between employees' production at work and their training and motivation.

TIP

For this 'identify' question, you just need to state the equation used to calculate productivity.

Activity 15.2

This activity will help you to demonstrate your understanding of inventory management.

The new operations director at the housebuilding firm B&L Homes wants to improve operational efficiency. One aspect of B&L that she is particularly interested in is stock management. She feels that the business holds too much stock, particularly raw materials and components such as bricks and cement. By reducing the firm's inventory levels, she feels that costs can be reduced and profits will rise.

a Outline the difference between inventories held as raw materials and components and inventories held as finished goods. **[4]**

b Identify **four** types of cost associated with holding inventories. **[4]**

c Explain **two** benefits to B&L of holding stock. **[6]**

Remember to make links here by showing, for example, the relationship between holding stock and the reduced risk of having to stop building a house if stock runs out.

d Do you think that B&L's decision to cut inventory levels will increase profits? Justify your answer. **[6]**

Start by setting out the benefits of reducing inventories such as that they will, for example, reduce costs such as warehousing space and then evaluate this by considering the benefits of holding stock.

Activity 15.3

Here, you have to show your knowledge and understanding of lean production.

Relax Sofa Company manufactures lounge furniture, such as sofas and chairs. The business adopted lean production three years ago and has seen its profits rise significantly as a result of the change. The key elements of the switch to lean production were the use of just-in-time inventory control and Kaizen. The employees have adapted well to the use of lean production because they are highly trained and very motivated.

a Define the term 'lean production'. **[2]**

b Identify **four** reasons for waste in a business such as Relax Sofa Company. **[4]**

c Outline **two** things that the Relax Sofa Company has to have in place to successfully use just-in-time production. **[4]**

Remember how, for example, just-in-time production can only function if stock is delivered when it is needed.

d Explain **one** reason why Kaizen might have improved quality and productivity at Relax Sofa Company. **[6]**

Activity 15.4

In this activity, you will need to apply your knowledge and understanding of different production methods.

Associated Bakeries PLC is a large bread manufacturing business. It's a high-performing business which achieves high levels of productivity. The bakeries operated as part of the business use batch production for manufacturing bread. Associated Bakeries also operates a specialist bakery that produces 'one-off' products such as cakes for special occasions. This bakery uses **job production** for this type of specialist work.

a State the difference between batch production and job production. **[4]**

b Outline why bread is often manufactured using **batch production**. **[6]**

Think about the stages of production that bread needs to go through when it is being produced.

c Explain why Associated Bakeries uses job production to produce cakes for special occasions. **[6]**

Here, you need to consider the types of cakes produced for special occasions such as weddings.

Activity 15.5

This set of questions covers the ways that technology affects production.

Tech Clean Ltd manufactures dishwashers for domestic and commercial use. The business has a new production plant in South America which opened six months ago. Tech Clean uses the very latest technology in the new plant with advanced computer-aided manufacturing (CAM) and computer-integrated manufacturing (CIM). The new plant's use of technology means that it employs 30% fewer employees, which has led to a significant reduction in Tech Clean's unit costs.

a Outline the difference between CAM and CIM. **[4]**

Think about the extent to which computers and robots can be used in Clean Tech's production process.

b Explain how the use of CAM has reduced Tech Clean's costs. **[6]**

c Do you think that businesses such as Tech Clean always benefit from new technology in production? Justify your answer. **[6]**

Start by developing your argument that technology benefits Tech Clean by, for example, improving the quality of the final product then evaluate this by, for example, looking at the cost of investing in technology.

Reflection: Now that you have worked on improving three sets of exam-style answers, think about the written quality of your own work. Do you feel that you are writing clear, concise answers, or do you need to focus on improving your writing style?

Learning summary

Before completing the activities in this unit, you should review your work on the following business topics:

- the different classifications of business costs
- the usefulness of cost data in business decision making
- economies and diseconomies of scale
- breakeven analysis.

KEY TERMS

Fixed costs: costs that do not change with output.

Variable costs: costs that change in direct proportion to output.

Total cost: all the variable and fixed costs of producing the total output.

Average costs: the cost of producing a single unit of output.

Economies of scale: the reduction in average costs as a result of increasing the scale of operations.

Activity 16.1

In this activity, you will be required to demonstrate what you have learnt about fixed and variable costs.

Table 16.1 sets out the costs of a business that manufactures t-shirts. Classify the costs listed as either fixed or variable costs.

Examples of costs	Fixed or variable costs
Insurance of capital equipment	
Cotton used to manufacture t shirts	
Salary of the marketing director	
Packaging used for the t-shirts	
Information labels attached to each t-shirt	
Rent of buildings	
Investment in production line machinery	
Production line workers' wages on piece rates	

Table 16.1

Activity 16.2

This question helps to develop your understanding of the relationship between costs and output using cost data.

Frame-it manufactures picture frames. It is a small, family-run organisation that supplies high-quality frames to art galleries and professional artists. Table 16.2 sets out the cost data for the business.

Output	Fixed cost	Variable cost $50 per frame	Total cost	Average cost
0	70 000			
10 000				
20 000				
30 000				
40 000				
50 000				

Table 16.2

a Outline the difference between a fixed and a variable cost. **[4]**

Think about how fixed and variable costs are affected by output.

b Calculate the fixed, variable, total and **average cost** at each level of output by completing the table. **[4]**

This 'calculate' question wants you to work out cost values from the given figures.

Be clear on your method for calculating the different costs and think about how realistic your cost figures are relative to the case study example.

c Explain why average costs fall as output increases. **[6]**

Think about the impact of fixed costs when calculating average costs.

Activity 16.3

In this activity, you are being asked to apply cost and revenue data to a business-decision-making situation.

The market for chewing gum is very competitive and T&Y Ltd's leading brands have proven to be loss-making. The CEO, Amit, thinks that Brand One should be discontinued but the marketing manager, Francesca, thinks that this would be a mistake. Cost and revenue data for two of its brands is set out in Table 16.3.

$'000s	Brand One	Brand Two	Total
Revenue	200	350	
Fixed cost	80	100	
Variable cost	130	160	
Total cost			
Profit			

Table 16.3

a Define the term '**total cost**'. **[2]**

b Calculate the total cost and profit for each brand and the total cost and profit for T&Y by completing the table. **[4]**

c Calculate the total profit for T&Y if it stopped producing Brand One but still had to cover the $80 000 fixed cost. **[4]**

Make sure that you consider the fixed costs of the discontinued brand when answering this question.

d Do you think that Amit is right to discontinue Brand One? Justify your answer. **[6]**

Activity 16.4

The aim of this activity is for you to show your knowledge of the different types of economy of scale.

Table 16.4 sets out examples of different **economies of scale**.

Complete the table by matching the examples with the following types of economy of scale:

- technical
- financial
- managerial
- purchasing
- marketing.

Example	Economy of scale
A major international airline gets a loan at a very low rate of interest.	
A pharmaceutical company invests in the latest CAM machinery.	
A major supermarket chain negotiates a deal to buy soft drinks from a supplier at a very low price.	
A large advertising agency divides its management into five specialist functions.	
A sports goods manufacturer divides its significant advertising budget by its very large output.	

Table 16.4

Activity 16.5

This activity is designed to help you practise your skills in applying the breakeven model.

Educate Ltd organises and manages conferences for the corporate sector. The business has grown significantly over the last five years and benefits from economies of scale which have reduced the average cost of holding events. However, there are now problems of communication and coordination as a result of Educate's growth. The costs and revenues for its next conference are set out in Table 16.5.

Item	Amount
Fixed cost	$70 000
Variable cost per delegate	$80
Ticket selling price	$220
Maximum delegate capacity	800
Target ticket sales	700

Table 16.5

a Identify **four** types of economy of scale that Educate might benefit from. **[4]**

b Consider how diseconomies of scale might be affecting Educate. **[4]**

You could develop the examples from the case study here.

c Consider the information in Table 16.5 and construct a breakeven chart for Educate's next conference. **[4]**

This question wants you to draw a diagram using a given set of figures. Make sure that you use graph paper and plot costs and revenues accurately. Remember to label all lines and axes clearly.

d Calculate the profit and the margin of safety of the next conference if Educate achieves its target sales. **[4]**

Show your working clearly when you are doing your calculations.

e Do you think that a breakeven diagram is a useful tool for managers when they are planning projects? Justify your answer. **[6]**

Reflection: In this unit, you should have developed an understanding of costs and revenues. How does your understanding of costs and revenues help you understand how businesses make decisions about price and output?

17 Achieving quality production

Learning summary

Before completing the activities in this unit, you should review your work on the following business topics:

- why **quality** is important to businesses
- **quality control**
- **quality assurance**.

KEY TERMS

Quality: ensuring a good or service that meets the needs and requirements of its consumer.

Quality standards: the minimum standard of production or service acceptable to consumers.

Quality control: checking the quality of goods through inspection.

Quality assurance: a system of setting agreed standards for every stage of production.

Activity 17.1

This activity introduces you to quality and why it is important.

Mugs-on-line Ltd manufactures and sells mugs, cups and plates through its own website. Customers use the business's online software to design their own products which are then delivered to customers within three days. The business is the market leader because of the quality of its products. Mugs-on-line uses the latest production technology and it makes sure that faults in production are minimised. One challenge is making sure that consumers get the exact product that they designed and ordered through the website.

a Define the term 'quality'. **[2]**

b State **two** ways that Mugs-on-line can achieve **quality standards** in the products that it produces. **[4]**

Consider the impact that labour and capital might have on quality at Mugs-on-line.

c Explain **two** reasons why quality is important to Mugs-on-line. **[6]**

The key thing here is to make the connection between quality and outcomes for Mugs-on-line, such as brand image.

TIP

Remember that an example from the case scenario is useful support for your definition.

Activity 17.2

This activity tests your understanding of quality and how it affects business performance.

There are problems at the Pizza Shack restaurant. Sales and profits have fallen significantly in the last year as customer satisfaction declined because of poor quality standards of food and service. The restaurant made a decision to try to reduce labour costs last year by hiring younger staff that they could pay lower wages to and by trying to run the restaurant with 15% fewer staff. This has had the effect of reducing staff motivation.

a Define the term 'quality standards'. **[2]**

Use precise terminology to define quality standards.

b Explain **two** reasons why a decline in quality at the Pizza Shack might lead to a fall in Pizza Shack's profits. **[6]**

It is important to make the connection between quality, revenues and costs in this question.

c Do you think that Pizza Shack's decision to cut labour costs by hiring younger staff and by having fewer staff was wrong? Justify your answer. **[6]**

Activity 17.3

The aim here is to help you check your understanding of quality control.

The quality control department at Agua Showers is under pressure. Agua Showers is a small business that manufactures high-quality showers that it fits and sells at a premium price. Quality is key to the business because customers paying the highest prices expect their showers to meet the very highest standards. There have been quality problems over the last two years and the manager of the quality control department has come under pressure because there is a feeling that the business should move towards quality assurance.

a State the difference between quality control and quality assurance. **[2]**

b Outline **two** problems for Agua Showers of using quality control. **[4]**

Think about, for example, the problems of only measuring quality at certain moments in the production process.

c Explain the impact that quality problems might have on Agua Showers's brand image. **[6]**

The nature of the market that Agua Showers operates in should give you a good clue about the importance of product quality for its brand image.

TIP
This 'explain' question is asking you to set out the relationships and reasons why and how quality assurance might lead to a fall in cost.

Activity 17.4

This activity gets you to show your evaluative skills and understanding of quality assurance.

The introduction of quality assurance at R&F Glass Ltd is seen as one of the key reasons for a 20% increase in the company's profits. This medium-sized business manufactures and fits double-glazed windows. One of the important benefits of introducing quality assurance has been improved quality standards. The windows have far fewer faults and this has significantly reduced costs.

a Identify **four** elements of quality assurance. **[4]**

b Explain why the use of quality assurance by R&F Glass might have led to a fall in its costs. **[6]**

c Do you think that R&F Glass was right to introduce quality assurance? Justify your answer. **[6]**

Reflection: What skills do you feel are most important when answering questions about quality control? Do you feel confident in using them? If not, why not?

18 Location decisions

Learning summary

Before completing the activities in this unit, you should review your work on the following business topics:

- what influences the location decision of manufacturing businesses and service businesses
- why businesses may decide to locate their operations in another country
- how legal controls affect location decisions.

KEY TERMS

Infrastructure: the basic facilities, services and installations needed for a business to function, for example, water, power, transport links.

Activity 18.1

This activity helps you to check your knowledge of quantitative and qualitative factors that affect location decisions by businesses.

Table 18.1 sets out the factors that affect a car manufacturer when deciding to locate a new manufacturing plant in Asia. Complete the table by stating whether the factor is a quantitative or a qualitative factor.

Example	Quantitative or qualitative factors
Cost of buying the site for the plant	
Availability and cost of local labour	
Size and position of the available site	
Legal restrictions	
Transport costs	
Local infrastructure issues	
Market potential in the region	
Government tax incentives	
Environmental and ethical considerations	

Table 18.1

Activity 18.2

These questions develop your understanding of how location decisions are made by businesses.

A crucial decision for OPure Ltd is where to locate its new bottled water plant. Its managers think that it is very important for OPure's future success to move to the north of the country. The new plant will enable the business to increase capacity by 20%. The town in the north of the country is seen as a good location for the new plant because it offers a low-cost site and a large and well-trained local labour force. There are, however, some concerns about the regional **infrastructure**.

a State the difference between quantitative and qualitative factors in OPure Ltd's location decision. **[2]**

b Explain how a low-cost site and a large and well-trained local labour force might affect Opure Ltd's location decision. **[6]**

Make the link between, for example, well-trained labour and how important that will be to OPure Ltd in producing its goods.

c Explain why concerns over the region's infrastructure might be a problem for OPure Ltd when it locates its new plant. **[6]**

Here, you need to think about OPure Ltd's operations and how these are affected by infrastructure. OPure Ltd will, for example, need to be able to transport its products to market efficiently.

Activity 18.3

TIP
This 'outline' question is asking you to clearly set out the main points relating to Crxpro's expansion into South America.

Choosing to expand overseas is a major decision for Crxpro Plc, which manufactures vacuum cleaners. The company's CEO, Alberta, sees a new manufacturing plant in Brazil as key to the future growth of the business. The city where Alberta wants to locate is seen as having significant advantages in terms of a low-cost labour force, good infrastructure and the opportunity to export to other South American markets.

a Define the term 'infrastructure'. **[2]**

b Outline **two** problems that Crxpro might encounter as it expands into South America. **[4]**

c Explain how Crxpro will benefit from the opportunity to export to other South American markets by locating in Brazil. **[6]**

Think about the benefit that locating in Brazil will give Crxpro by being able to increase sales in South America.

d Do you think that Crxpro's potential expansion into overseas markets is a good decision? Justify your answer. **[6]**

Start your answer by considering the benefits of expanding into Brazil and evaluate this by looking at some of the challenges such as cultural differences.

Activity 18.4

TIP
This 'justify' question is asking you to develop an argument about the problems of Besure locating overseas based on evidence.

Besure Insurance has decided to move out of London and locate in Paris. Many of the business's employees are unhappy about moving because it means relocating to another country. There are also some important legal constraints associated with the move. A number of Besure's employees will need work visas. The new office is based on an industrial park and there have been significant problems with securing an office leasing contract because of French commercial property regulations.

a Identify **four** areas of business that might be affected by legal controls. **[4]**

b Outline how obtaining work visas and a lease contract in France is important to Besure. **[6]**

Be clear on why these legal documents are needed by Besure when it locates to Paris.

c Explain the impact that relocating its employees to Paris might have on Besure's performance. **[6]**

d Do you think that the problems of locating overseas should stop Besure deciding to locate in Paris? Justify your answer. **[6]**

Build this answer by setting out some of the problems of relocation and evaluate these by considering the benefits of relocation, such as accessing a new market.

Reflection: Think about all aspects of business location that you have learnt about and how this influences business decision making. Which aspects are you most comfortable explaining, and why? Which ones do you need to practise more?

Exam-style practice questions

All exam-style practice questions and sample answers in this title were written by the author(s). In examinations, the way marks are awarded may be different.

Expanding into Eastern Europe is a key decision for R&C speakers. The business has operated successfully in Spain for ten years. The next part of its strategic development is to move to a new manufacturing plant near Warsaw in Poland. The finance director has produced the forecast data in the table.

Cost, revenue, output	
Fixed cost	$825 000
Variable cost (per speaker)	$25
Selling price	$80
Maximum output (speakers)	20 000

The new manufacturing plant will use the latest technology using computer-integrated manufacturing. It will also use just-in-time inventory management.

a Define the term 'computer-integrated manufacturing'. **[2]**

b Outline **two** location factors that could have affected R&C's decision to locate near Warsaw. **[2]**

c Consider the data in the table and construct a breakeven diagram for R&C's new manufacturing plant showing the breakeven quantity. **[4]**

d Explain **two** factors that have to be in place for R&C to successfully use just-in-time inventory management. **[6]**

e Do you think that R&C will benefit from locating its new manufacturing plant in Warsaw? Justify your answer. **[6]**

Total available marks: 20

Exam-style case study

The Cabin Company

It is an important year for The Cabin Company as it decides where to locate its new factory as part of its expansion plans. The business manufactures wooden cabins for consumers and industrial markets. The Cabin Company is a US-based business that appointed a new CEO, George, two years ago. He has managed significant changes to the businesses operations. He wanted to improve the business's productivity and saw the introduction of lean production methods as a key part of this.

George also wanted to grow the business to benefit from economies of scale. Part of this expansion is opening a new factory. The Cabin Company is considering two locations and the financial and qualitative information is set out in Appendix 1.

Another key objective for George is to improve the quality of The Cabin Company's products. The business has decided to replace quality control with quality assurance and this has resulted in improvement in the quality of the business's product. To achieve the goal of improving quality, George has stressed the importance of recruiting the best-quality employees.

Appendix 1

Information about locations for a new factory

	Location 1	Location 2
Breakeven output	3500	4800
Forecast profit	$7 000 000	$6 500 000
Infrastructure links	Some weaknesses	Generally good
Availability of skilled labour	Some limitations	Very good availability

1 a Explain **four** ways that The Cabin Company could improve its productivity.

Method 1:
Explanation:

Method 2:
Explanation:

Method 3:
Explanation:

Method 4:
Explanation:

[8]

b Explain the benefits to The Cabin Company of the introduction of lean production:

- Quality is improved.
- The cost of holding inventories is minimised.
- Unit costs are reduced.

Which benefit do you think is **most** significant? Justify your answer.

Quality:
Reduction of holding inventory cost:
Reduction of unit costs:
Conclusion:

[12]

2 a Explain **four** different types of economies of scale that The Cabin Company might benefit from.

Type 1:
Explanation:

Type 2:
Explanation:

Type 3:
Explanation:

Type 4:
Explanation:

[8]

b Explain the following benefits to The Cabin Company of using breakeven analysis:

- easy to construct and interpret
- provides financial information that The Cabin Company can use to determine the target output
- can show the effect on a decision of a change in costs and revenues.

Which do you think is the **most** important benefit? Justify your answer.

Easy to construct and interpret:
Financial information to determine target output:
Shows effect on a decision of a change in cost and revenues:
Conclusion:

[12]

3 a Explain **two** aspects of The Cabin Company's change to quality assurance from quality control.

Aspect 1:
Explanation:

Aspect 2:
Explanation:

[8]

b Explain how improving quality would affect The Cabin Company's:

- brand image
- costs.

Which do you think would have the **most** effect on profit? Justify your answer.

Brand image:
Costs:
Conclusion:

[12]

4 a Explain **two** qualitative factors that The Cabin Company might take into account when it chooses the location of its new factory.

Factor 1:
Explanation:

Factor 2:
Explanation:

[8]

b Consider the cost and revenue data along with the non-financial information in Appendix 1 for the **two** possible locations for The Cabin Company's new factory.

Using financial and non-financial information, which factory should The Cabin Company choose? Justify your answer.

Financial information:

Non-financial information:

Conclusion:

[12]

Total marks available: 80

Answering exam-style practice question d

Here is a sample answer to exam-style practice question d. The answer contains some common weaknesses. Read each part and consider how the answer could be improved.

Just-in-time inventory management (JIT) means that stock arrives at R&C when it is needed for production [K] so that stock holding is minimised by the business. For JIT to be successful, R&C must have good relationships with its suppliers of raw materials and components [App]. This is because inventories have to be delivered on time. If they are not, production may be interrupted and the business may not be able to supply speakers to its customers [An]. The next factor for JIT to be successful is the need for R&C's employees to be flexible so that they can make the stock management system work effectively.

Improve the answer...

There are some ways to improve this answer. Did you think about these?

The first part of this answer is strong because it clearly sets out the importance of good relationships with suppliers and makes good references to the case study business. The points about interrupted production and failing to supply producers are particularly good.

The second part of the answer is weak because it fails to explain the importance of flexible employees to the effective operation of JIT. The answer could stress how workers must be able to switch to the production of a different product when new stocks of speaker components arrive.

Answering exam-style case study question 4b

Here is a sample answer to exam-style case study question 4b. The answer contains some common weaknesses. Read each part and consider how the answer could be improved.

Financial information: Appendix 1 has the breakeven point for location 1 at 3500 units whereas it is 4800 for location 2. The higher breakeven point for location 2 gives it the advantage. Location 1, however, has a higher forecast profit, which makes it better to choose location 1 [App]. These are, however, forecast figures and there could be some difference when the location actually takes place.

Non-financial information: Location 2 is better than location 1 on infrastructure links, which means that there are good road and rail links, which would be better for The Cabin Company [App]. Location 2 has much better availability of skilled labour than location 1 and this could be crucial to The Cabin Company if it wants to achieve the quality that George wants to achieve [An].

Conclusion: With the better breakeven figures, infrastructure links and the availability of skilled labour, location 1 is the best option for the business despite the lower forecast profit [Ev].

Improve the answer...

There are some ways to improve this answer. Did you think about these?

There is a weak start to this answer because the response shows a misunderstanding of breakeven, because the higher breakeven figure is not an advantage of location 2 but a disadvantage relative to location 1. The interpretation of the profit figure is correct and location 1 is seen as having the advantage. There is a good point on the problems of using forecast data. The answer accurately considers the advantage that location 2 has on infrastructure, although this could be more fully explained by discussing the benefit of good infrastructure such as being able to get inventory into the factory and finished goods out to the market in an efficient way. The point about the availability of skilled labour is well made with its reference to George's aim of needing skilled labour to improve the business's quality. The final conclusion is logical but does not fully explain why the other factory is ruled out.

Section 5
Financial information and decisions

19 Business finance: needs and sources

Learning summary

Before completing the activities in this unit, you should review your work on the following business topics:

- why businesses need finance
- the difference between **short-term** and **long-term finance**
- the main sources of finance
- how businesses make financial choices.

KEY TERMS

Start-up cost: the capital needed by an entrepreneur when first starting a business.

Non-current (fixed) assets: resources owned by a business which will be used for a period longer than one year.

Long-term finance: debt or equity used to finance the purchase of **non-current assets** or to finance expansion plans.

Short-term finance: loans of debt that a business expects to pay back within one year.

Retained profit: profit remaining after all expenses, tax and dividends have been paid, and which is put back into the business.

Mortgage: a long-term loan used for the purchase of land or buildings.

Equity finance: permanent finance provided by the owners of a limited company.

Activity 19.1

This activity will help you to apply your understanding of why businesses need finance.

It has been six months since Maria resigned from her job in banking and started her own flower stall at a major train station in Copenhagen. Maria put in $20 000 of her own savings and also took out a $30 000 bank loan. Her major **start-up cost** included capital expenditure on a high-quality stall and a computer system for processing receipts and payments. She also needed funds to cover stock purchases.

a Identify **four** reasons why businesses need finance. **[4]**

b Define the term 'capital expenditure'. **[2]**

c Outline **two** types of payment that Maria will need to pay to the bank for taking the $30 000 bank loan. **[4]**

Think about the ongoing cost of any loan and what the lender will eventually need once the loan has run its course.

d Explain **two** reasons why businesses like Maria's might find it difficult to raise finance. **[6]**

Think about why Maria's flower stall, as a small business, represents a risk to a lender and link this to the problem of raising finance.

Activity 19.2

This activity helps you to consider the types of finance that businesses can use.

It has been a record year for Blue Loch fish farm. Revenue has increased by 20% in the last 12 months and profits are up 18%. Blue Loch now has the opportunity to purchase a new farm 7 miles away which would double the business's capacity. The $6 million cost of the new farm is partly funded by **retained profits** and partly funded by a **mortgage**. The business is concerned about the high interest cost associated with the mortgage.

a Outline the difference between short-term and long-term finance. **[4]**

It is useful to consider why businesses want long- or short-term finance.

b Explain **one** advantage and **one** disadvantage that Blue Loch might have from using retained profits to fund the purchase of the new farm. **[6]**

Remember, for example, that retained profit is not borrowed so it is not subject to the costs of borrowed finance.

c Do you think that Blue Loch should take out the loan to fund the new fish farm? Justify your answer. **[6]**

TIP

This 'justify' question is asking you to have a discussion that leads to a conclusion on Blue Loch taking out the loan.

Activity 19.3

This activity will require you to apply your knowledge of the different types of finance.

Table 19.1 sets out examples of finance raised by a mining business.

Match the following types of finance to the examples given in the table:

- trade receivables
- debt factoring
- bank loan
- leasing
- mortgage
- debenture issue
- **equity finance.**

Example	Type of finance
The business issued $40m of new shares last year.	
A major industrial customer owes the mining business $1.5m.	
The business plans to sell $10m of bonds next year.	
A finance company has loaned the firm $14m to purchase a new building which is secured against the value of the building.	
The mining business sells $1m of trade receivables to a finance company.	
The mining business uses a fleet of company vehicles which it pays $1.7m per year to use.	
The business has signed an agreement of $2.5m from the bank to purchase a new drilling machine.	

Table 19.1

Activity 19.4

Here, you are expected to answer questions on funding for a small business.

Breaking into the Nigerian clothing market was always going to be difficult for Fantasy Socks. The idea of brightly patterned socks had been developed by Fatoumata when she was at university and, along with her friend Abieyuwa, they had an exciting business concept. The problem was funding. With very little of their own money and the banks being reluctant to lend to them, they were considering micro-finance and crowd funding.

a Define the term 'micro-finance'. **[2]**

b Explain how Fantasy Socks could use e-commerce to raise money through crowd funding. **[6]**

c Why do you think that small businesses are always going to find it difficult to raise finance? Justify your answer. **[6]**

Start your answer by explaining why small businesses have problems raising finance, such as their lack of existing finance. This can be evaluated by considering the opportunities that small businesses offer to banks as borrowers.

Activity 19.5

This set of questions focuses on cash flow and liquidity.

The directors at the department store Henry's held several crisis meetings to decide how they were going to cover a $3.5 million liquidity problem. The business had just received a large tax bill and several suppliers were demanding immediate payment. Their cash-flow problem had been building for three years. The growth in online shopping had reduced their sales revenue and increases in the minimum wage had increased their costs. The directors' plan was to sell an additional $5m of shares to a major investor. Renee, Henry's CEO, was cautious about the deal because it would mean losing some control of the business.

TIP

This 'explain' question wants you to set out why and how Henry's got into cash-flow difficulties.

a Identify **four** factors influencing the choice of finance for a business. **[4]**

b Explain how Henry's had got into cash-flow difficulties. **[6]**

c Outline **two** sources of funds, other than share issue, that Henry's could access to fund its liquidity problems. **[4]**

d Do you think that Henry's should sell the $5m share issue to the outside investor? Justify your answer. **[6]**

It is important to consider the benefits of the share issue and then move on to discuss the disadvantages of using equity finance, such as a possible loss of decision-making control.

Reflection: Think about what you have learnt about the types of finance available to businesses. Can you confidently analyse what types of finance a business might choose and why? If not, how can you improve?

20 Cash-flow forecasting and working capital

Learning summary

Before completing the activities in this unit, you should review your work on the following business topics:

- the importance of cash to businesses
- **cash-flow forecasting**
- how businesses deal with short-term cash-flow problems
- the importance of working capital to business.

KEY TERMS

Cash-flow forecast: an estimate of the future cash inflows and outflows of a business.

Net cash flow: cash inflow minus cash outflow.

Liquidity: the ability of a business to pay its short-term debts.

Working capital: the capital needed to finance the day-to-day running expenses and pay the short-term debts of a business.

Activity 20.1

These questions check your knowledge and understanding of the importance of cash flow to a business.

Things are getting difficult for Chinese catering supplier The Hot Wok. Based in a southern city in China, the business supplies food for corporate customers and major events. The business has done well for the last five years but things are tough at the moment because a major customer has gone bankrupt and failed to pay a $600 000 debt. This has put The Hot Wok's cash flow under considerable pressure and forced it to adapt its cash-flow forecast for next year.

a Identify **four** items that The Hot Wok would need cash for. **[4]**

b Outline how The Hot Wok would have produced its cash-flow forecast. **[4]**

c Explain why the failure of the customer to pay its $600 000 debt is a problem for The Hot Wok's cash flow. **[6]**

Here, you need to make the connection between paying a significant debt and cash outflows from The Hot Wok.

Activity 20.2

This activity develops your skill in producing a cash-flow forecast and interpreting it.

The finance director of Cool-it Ltd is putting together the business's cash-flow forecast for the coming year. The Australian-based business's sales are growing strongly and there is a need to manage cash flow carefully. It is particularly important to manage trade receivables carefully. Table 20.1 sets out an incomplete cash-flow forecast for Cool-it Ltd for the coming year.

$'000s	Jan	Feb	Mar	Apr	May	Jun
Cash inflow						
Receipts	18	18	20	21	22	23
Total inflow						
Cash outflow						
Payments	12	22	13	18	15	16
Total outflow						
Net cash flow	**6**	**(4)**	**7**	3	A	B
Opening balance	4	10	6	C	D	E
Closing balance	**10**	6	13	F	G	H

Table 20.1

a Define the term '**net cash flow**'. **[2]**

b Calculate the missing cash-flow figures in the table by filling in A–H. **[4]**

Calculate the net cash flow, the opening balance and the closing balance in the table by working methodically through each month and remembering that the figures affect each other.

c Explain why an increase in Cool-it Ltd's sales leads to a rise in its cash outflows. **[6]**

Make the link between the payments needed to pay for stock as sales rise and cash outflows.

TIP
Make sure that you carefully follow the cash-flow figures through the forecast in the table because one figure determines the next figure.

Activity 20.3

The aim here is to further develop your skill in producing a cash-flow forecast and your understanding of negative cash-flow situations.

It has been a tough year for Square Box Ltd as a result of cash-flow problems. Square Box makes and sells cardboard boxes for industrial customers. Sales are falling and this has led to a significant decline in the business's **liquidity** position. A key problem that the business faces is customers who are slow to pay, which has made its working capital cycle difficult to manage.

$'000s	Jan	Feb	Mar	Apr	May	Jun
Cash inflow						
Receipts	31	29	29	27	25	22
Total inflow						
Cash outflow						
Payments	24	33	23	22	29	21
Total outflow						
Net cash flow	**7**	B	6	F	(4)	1
Opening balance	A	2	D	4	G	5
Closing balance	**2**	C	E	9	5	H

Table 20.2

a Outline the working capital cycle for a business. **[4]**

b Calculate the missing cash-flow figures in Table 20.2. **[4]**

c Consider how Square Box might finance with the negative cash-flow position in February. **[4]**

Reflect on the sources of finance from the previous unit.

d Explain why Square Box's customers who are slow to pay might make the business's working capital cycle difficult to manage. **[6]**

Start by setting out the working capital cycle and make the connection between the flow of funds in the working capital cycle and slow-paying customers.

Activity 20.4

This activity gets you to consider the link between cash flow, liquidity and significant investment.

The board of directors at Fix-it Ltd, a chain of DIY stores in Canada, wants to update the organisation's IT system. This is a major investment for the organisation of $1.6m, which represents a significant proportion of its sales revenue. The business has a manageable liquidity position but it is going to use $600 000 of cash to invest in the project, which will put liquidity under pressure. It has arranged a $1m loan to fund the rest of the investment, but this will put pressure on future liquidity. One way of improving the situation is to delay payment to suppliers by a few days to hold cash in the business for longer.

a Define the term 'liquidity'. **[2]**

b Outline the effect that the $600 000 cash used to fund the IT investment at Fix-it will have on its liquidity position. **[4]**

c Explain why a loan taken out to fund the investment in the IT system will affect Fix-it's future cash flow. **[6]**

Consider the two future payments that have to be made when a business borrows money and connect this to cash flow.

d Given Fix-it's liquidity position, do you think that it is right to invest in the new IT system? Justify your answer. **[6]**

TIP

You need to make a judgement about the importance of liquidity to Fix-it in this 'justify' question.

Reflection: These questions involve cash-flow calculations. How well have you learnt the technique for producing cash-flow forecasts? Are you more confident when interpreting cash-flow data or can you think of areas you'd like to improve?

Learning summary

Before completing the activities in this unit, you should review your work on the following business topics:

- the importance of **profit**
- how profit is calculated
- the difference between profit and cash
- **income statements**.

KEY TERMS

Gross profit: the difference between revenue and cost of sales.

Profit: the difference between revenue and total costs.

Total cost: costs of sales plus expenses.

Revenue: the amount earned from the sale of products.

Cost of sales: the cost of purchasing the goods used to make the products sold.

Expenses: day-to-day operating expenses of a business.

Income statement: a financial statement which records the revenue, costs and profits of a business for a given period of time.

Activity 21.1

This set of questions helps to develop your understanding of revenue, costs and profits.

Spyros is the finance director of the Greek food production company Tróei. He has been asked to do a presentation to the board of directors at Tróei on this year's financial results. The key aspects of his presentation are:

- 10% increase in **gross profit**
- 5% increase in **profit**
- 8% increase in **total cost**
- 12% increase in **revenue.**

a Identify **four** types of **expenses** which make up Tróei's total cost. **[4]**

b Outline the difference between profit and gross profit. **[4]**

Think about how different types of cost are used to calculate different profit figures.

c Outline **two** reasons why Tróei's revenue might have increased. **[4]**

To answer this, consider how revenue is calculated.

d Explain why a rise in Tróei's revenue might lead to a rise in its **cost of sales**. **[6]**

Analyse the link between the number of units that Tróei sells and how this affects the cost of sales.

Activity 21.2

The aim of this activity is to test your skills in calculating profit and explaining data in an income statement.

Pure fruit trading buys and sells mangoes and is based in Pakistan. Noor, the business's finance director, has collected the following data for Pure fruit trading for the first six months of this year. The selling price of the mangoes is $4.

	Jan	Feb	Mar	Apr	May	Jun
Units sold	9000	11 000	10 000	8000	10 000	12 000
Revenue						
Cost of sales	$18 000	$22 000	$20 000	$16 000	$20 000	$24 000
Gross profit						
Expenses	$12 000	$12 000	$12 000	$12 000	$12 000	$12 000
Profit						

Table 21.1

a Define the term 'cost of sales'. **[2]**

b Calculate Pure fruit trading's monthly revenue for each of the first six months. **[2]**

c Calculate Pure fruit trading's monthly gross profit for each of the first six months. **[2]**

d Calculate Pure fruit trading's monthly profit for each of the first six months. **[2]**

Think carefully about your method in each of these calculation questions and show your working.

e Explain why the expenses figure of $12 000 has remained constant over the first six months. **[6]**

Remember the nature of expenses and how their behaviour is or is not affected by changes in output.

TIP

These 'calculate' questions want you to work out revenue and profit values from the data given.

Activity 21.3

This activity provides an opportunity for you to apply your understanding and make judgements about income data from different companies.

The face cream business in an economy is extremely competitive. There are three major cosmetic producers – Ice Plc, Shine Skin Plc and So-Pure Plc. The cost, revenue and profit data of each producer is set out in Table 21.2.

$m	Ice Plc	Shine Skin Plc	So-Pure Plc
Revenue	123	98	143
Cost of sales	43	31	74
Gross profit			
Expenses	56	46	24
Net profit			

Table 21.2

a State how revenue is calculated in Table 21.2. **[2]**

b Calculate the gross profit for each business. **[2]**

c Calculate the net profit for each business. **[2]**

d Do you think that So-Pure is the best-performing business of the businesses in the table? Justify your answer. **[6]**

Activity 21.4

In this activity, you need to show your knowledge of how information in the income statement relates to different stakeholders.

Table 21.3 sets out examples of the interests of different stakeholders in an organisation. Match each example to its type of stakeholder:

- shareholders
- employees
- lenders
- government
- suppliers
- managers.

Example	Stakeholders
The high profits of a business have driven up its share price.	
The losses of a business mean that it might have to make redundancies.	
The losses of a business mean that it might struggle to pay for stock.	
The net profit of a business is used to calculate its tax.	
The high profit of a business means a bonus for the business's leadership.	
The losses of a business mean that it may not be able to pay its debts.	

Table 21.3

TIP

This 'outline' question needs clear statements on the difference between cash and profit.

Activity 21.5

This activity aims to develop your understanding of the relationship between profit and cash flow.

Dry Form Towels is a Turkish-based towel manufacturer. The business's sales are rising and it is profitable but it is suffering cash-flow problems. As a small business, Dry Form buys raw materials from a large supplier of cotton and the supplier gives Dry Form a short credit period. Some of its customers, however, take a long time to pay.

a Outline **two** reasons why cash and profit might differ in a business. **[4]**

Think about the difference between the times when profit and cash flow are recorded.

b Explain why the short credit period of Dry Form's supplier is causing it cash-flow problems. **[6]**

Try to relate the timing of cash received from customers and cash payments made to suppliers.

c Do you think that Dry Form should make its customers pay more quickly? Justify your answer. **[6]**

Reflection: Consider what you have learnt about the ways that revenue, costs, profit and cash are recorded in the income statement. What skills have you developed to help you to interpret income?

22 Statement of financial position

Learning summary

Before completing the activities in this unit, you should review your work on the following business topics:

- the main parts of a statement of financial position
- **assets** and **liabilities**
- how to interpret a simple statement of financial position.

KEY TERMS

Assets: resources that are owned by a business.

Liabilities: debts of the business that will have to be paid sometime in the future.

Non-current (fixed) assets: resources that a business owns and expects to use for more than one year.

Current assets: resources that the business owns and expects to convert into cash before the date of the next statement of financial position.

Current liabilities: debts of the business which it expects to pay before the date of the next statement of financial position.

Non-current liabilities: debts of the business which will be payable after more than one year.

Owner's equity: the amount owed by the business to its owners, including capital and retained profits.

Shareholder's equity (funds): alternative term for owner's equity, but can only be used by limited liability companies.

Activity 22.1

This question checks your understanding of the basic make-up of the statement of financial position.

Tall Trees Ltd is a chain of garden centres and it is planning to buy (take over) a family garden centre called Dry Hill Ltd. The financial director at Tall Trees has spent time analysing Dry Hill's statement of financial position whilst deciding on whether to buy Dry Hill. The statement of financial position values Dry Hill at $14m.

a Define the term 'statement of financial position'. **[2]**

b Identify **four** types of asset that might be in Dry Hill's statement of financial position. **[4]**

c Explain how Dry Hill's buildings and inventories would have been valued. **[6]**

Consider how you might value a building and an item of stock.

Activity 22.2

In this activity, you are expected to show your knowledge of the different items in the statement of financial position.

Table 22.1 sets out examples of the following items in the statement of financial position for a mobile phone manufacturer:

- **non-current asset**
- **current asset**, **current liability**
- **non-current liability**
- **owner's equity**.

Match each of the examples with the different items in the statement of financial position.

Example	Statement item
Retained profit	
Shares issued by the business	
Mobile phone manufacturing equipment	
Building used for production	
Money owed to the business by its customers	
The business's overdraft	
Money owed by the business to its suppliers	
Cash in the bank	
Debentures issued by the business	
Stock of components used to manufacture the phones	

Table 22.1

Activity 22.3

The aim of this activity is to develop your understanding of the different components in the statement of financial position.

It has been a good year for En Chocolat, a Ghanaian chocolate manufacturer. Sales are up nearly 50% over the last two years and this has led to a 30% increase in retained profits. One issue of the growth in sales is a significant increase in the inventories that En Chocolat has to hold. En Chocolat's statement of financial position is set out in Table 22.2.

$'000s	Year 1	Year 2
Non-current (fixed) assets		400
Current assets	200	
Less:		
Current liabilities	A	
Net current assets		80
Net assets		B
Financed by:		
Owner's capital (equity)		360
Non-current (long-term) liabilities		C
Capital employed		D

Table 22.2

TIP

Remember how the figures in the statement of financial position are related to each other when you are answering numerical questions on this topic.

a Outline the difference between current liabilities and long-term liabilities. **[4]**

b Calculate En Chocolat's statement of financial position by completing the missing figures in fields A–D in Table 22.2. **[4]**

Focus on how the figures in the statement of financial position are related to each other.

c Explain how En Chocolat's statement of financial position is affected by the increase in inventories. **[6]**

You need to make the connection between inventories, current assets and net assets here.

d Explain how a 30% increase in En Chocolat's profit would affect its statement of financial position. **[6]**

Remember the relationship between profit and owner's equity in this question.

Activity 22.4

The questions in this activity develop your understanding of how the statement of financial position is important to stakeholders.

Clear Ver Ltd manufactures all types of glasses from reading glasses to sunglasses. The business wants to secure an extra $20m of funding from a major commercial bank to fund further expansion. Clear Ver is successful but the bank is concerned about the existing borrowing that the business already has and the additional interest payments that Clear Ver will have to make on its new borrowing. Clear Ver's statement of financial position for the last two years is set out in Table 22.3.

	2016	$'000s	2018	$'000s
Fixed assets				
Tangible fixed assets				
Buildings	14 000		14 000	
Machinery	10 000		12 000	
Equipment	6000		9000	
		A		B
Current assets				
Inventories	1500		1800	
Trade (accounts) receivables	500		600	
Cash and bank balance	C		300	
Total		2400		2700
Current liabilities				
Overdraft	400		700	
Trade (accounts) payables	600		D	
Short-term loan	100	1100	200	1600
Net current asset		1300		1100
Net asset		31 300		E
Equity				

(Continued)

	2016	$'000s	2018	$'000s
Share capital	25 000		25 000	
Retained profit	13 000		17 900	
Total		38 000		42 900
Long-term liabilities		6700		6700
Capital employed		F		36 100

Table 22.3

a Calculate the missing figures for fields A–F in Table 22.3. **[6]**

Be careful to show the relationship between the different figures in the statement of financial position.

b Outline why the asset value of machinery might have increased from 2016 to 2017. **[4]**

c Explain **two** reasons why the retained profit figure in **shareholder's equity** for Clear Ver might have increased from 2016 to 2017. **[6]**

'Explain' questions are looking for you to make links to show how and why things happen.

d Do you think that the bank that is considering making a loan to Clear Ver should be concerned about Clear Ver's existing borrowing? Justify your answer. **[6]**

Reflection: How confident are you about making connections between a statement of financial position and the performance of a business? What skills do you feel that you could improve to make your understanding clearer?

23 Analysis of accounts

Learning summary

Before completing the activities in this unit, you should review your work on the following business topics:

- profitability ratios and liquidity ratios
- the importance of **liquidity**
- why and how accounts are used.

KEY TERMS

Gross profit margin %: ratio between gross profit and revenue.

Profit margin %: ratio between profit before tax and revenue.

Return on capital employed (ROCE): ratio between profit before tax and capital employed.

Liquidity: the ability of a business to pay its short-term debts.

Current ratio: ratio between current assets and current liabilities.

Acid test ratio: ratio between liquid assets and current liabilities.

Activity 23.1

This activity develops your understanding of the basic principles of measuring business performance.

Table 23.1 sets out financial data for Malibu Inc, a US-based advertising agency. The company is struggling and a number of its key stakeholders are concerned about the prospects for business in the future. New competition in the market is putting pressure on Malibu Inc's revenues.

$m	2015	2016	2017
Revenue	850	810	740
Profit	120	105	90
Total equity	720	740	770

Table 23.1

a State how you would calculate total equity. **[2]**

Think about the funds that are attributable to the owners/shareholders of Malibu Inc.

TIP

This 'state' question is asking you to set out how you would calculate total equity.

b Explain why total equity might have risen from 2015 to 2017. **[6]**

It is important to focus on retained profit here.

c Do you think that Malibu's performance has got worse over the three years? Justify your answer. **[6]**

Consider the importance of the link between performance and profit and revenue and then evaluate this by discussing other factors that affect performance such as business efficiency.

Activity 23.2

This set of questions will help you to check your understanding of and ability to apply the ratios gross profit margin, profit margin and return on capital employed.

Table 23.2 sets out financial data for two of the leading businesses in tutoring and education in Argentina. Aprender Inc and Escucha Inc are both performing well in a market that is growing strongly. Total market sales have increased by 12% in each of the last two years. Both companies are hoping to raise new finance and potential investors are very interested in each business's performance.

$m	Aprender	Escucha
Revenue	34	15
Gross profit	19	8
Profit before tax and interest	5	4
Capital employed	12	9

Table 23.2

a State the equations for **gross profit margin** and **profit margin**. **[2]**

b Calculate gross profit margin, profit margin and **return on capital employed**. **[6]**

Make sure that you show your working carefully.

c Explain which business has performed the best in terms of return on capital employed. **[6]**

You need to make the connection between the value of both businesses' return on capital employed figures and their respective performances.

d Do you think that financial ratios are a good way for stakeholders to make judgements about the performance of Aprender and Escucha? Justify your answer. **[6]**

Activity 23.3

This set of questions focuses on the use of ratios to measure a business's liquidity.

Things are very difficult at Encore Ltd. The musical instrument manufacturing company is in the middle of a significant liquidity crisis following poor trading conditions. Sales of Encore's instruments are falling because of cheap competition from overseas and because of a weak domestic economy. Encore's cash-flow problems have been made worse since one of its major customers went bankrupt owing Encore a significant amount of money.

$'000s	2016	2017
Current assets	28	19
Inventories	16	14
Current liabilities	14	11

Table 23.3

a State the equations for the **current ratio** and the **acid test ratio**. **[2]**

TIP

This is a 'state' question so you just need to write the equations here.

b Calculate the current ratio and the acid test ratio for Encore. **[4]**

c Outline what Encore's current ratio and acid test ratio tell you about the business's liquidity. **[4]**

d Explain why the bankruptcy of Encore's major customer and the weak domestic economy might have led to liquidity problems at Encore. **[6]**

Focus on consequences for Encore's liquidity of not receiving a significant amount of cash from a customer.

Activity 23.4

The aim of this set of questions is to use ratio analysis on the statement of financial position and income statement to judge a business's performance.

It has been an important year for Spinning Blade Company, which is fighting hard to grow its market share in the renewable energy market. The business manufactures components for wind turbines in Malaysia and is seen as producing a high-value-added product. The business has just invested $110 000 in new machinery and has financed this through a loan and existing cash generated by retained profit. Table 23.4 shows Spinning Blade's statement of financial position and Table 23.5 sets out its income statement.

Statement of financial position		
$'000s	2016	2017
Non-current (fixed) assets	400	510
Current assets	80	70
Less:		
Current liabilities	50	60
Net current assets	30	10
Net assets	430	460
Financed by:		
Owner's capital (equity)	310	320
Non-current (long-term) liabilities	120	200
Capital employed	430	520

Table 23.4

Income statement		
$'000s	2016	2017
Revenue	350	420
Cost of sales	210	230
Gross profit	140	190
Expenses	90	100
Profit	50	90

Table 23.5

a Outline what producing a high-value-added product means for Spinning Blade Company. **[4]**

b Using Spinning Blade's income statement and statement of financial position, calculate the following ratios for 2016 and 2017:

- gross profit margin
- profit margin
- return on capital employed. **[6]**

Do not forget to set out your calculations carefully and show your working.

c Outline what the gross profit margin and the profit margin say about Spinning Blade's performance from 2016 to 2017. **[4]**

d Calculate the current ratio and explain the impact that the business growth from 2016 to 2017 has had on Spinning Blade's liquidity. **[6]**

e Do you think that financial ratios are a good way of judging Spinning Blade's performance? Justify your answer. **[6]**

Reflection: What have you learnt about structuring longer answers? Are there ways that you can improve your approach?

All exam-style practice questions and sample answers in this title were written by the author(s). In examinations, the way marks are awarded may be different.

Exam-style practice questions

Tariq, the new CEO at casual shoe manufacturer Canvas Ltd, is looking to improve the business's profitability. He is concerned about rising costs and the negative impact that these have had on Canvas Ltd. He wants to reduce the business's cost of sales to improve Canvas Ltd's value added. The table shows the income statement for Canvas in 2016 and 2017.

Income statement		
$'000s	2016	2017
Revenue	170	180
Cost of sales	90	210
Gross profit	A	70
Expenses	60	B
Profit	20	5

a Define the term 'gross profit'. **[2]**

b Calculate A and B from Canvas Ltd's income statement. **[2]**

c Outline **two** ways that Canvas Ltd could reduce its cost of sales. **[4]**

d Explain **two** ways that Canvas Ltd could increase its revenues. **[6]**

e Do you think that Canvas Ltd's performance has deteriorated over the period? Justify your answer, using appropriate ratios. **[6]**

Total available marks: 20

Exam-style case study

The Reel Cinema Ltd

The New Zealand-based cinema chain The Reel Cinema Ltd has seen growth over the last three years. The numbers attending the cinema complex have been rising quite steadily but different stakeholders, particularly The Reel Cinema's shareholders, have been concerned by the business's profitability. Appendix 1 sets out data used to produce The Reel Cinema's income statement for the last three years.

Louise is the finance director at The Reel Cinema and she is concerned about the firm's cash-flow position. Louise has produced a cash-flow forecast for the first three months of the coming year and the data for this is set out in Appendix 2. The opening cash balance for The Reel Cinema at the start of the year is $2000.

Some of the business's lenders are concerned about its liquidity position. The Reel Cinema's current and acid test ratios are set out in Appendix 3.

The views of the lenders are seen as important at this time as Louise has produced a finance proposal to fund investment in the latest screening technology. The business is looking at the following options to fund the investment: retained profit, leasing, or a bank loan.

Appendix 1

Income statement for The Reel Cinema Ltd

	2015	2016	2017
Revenue	$210 000	$222 000	$256 000
Cost of sales	$120 000	$135 000	$167 000
Gross profit	A	C	E
Expenses	$62 000	$67 000	$81 000
Profit	B	D	F

Appendix 2

Cash-flow forecast for The Reel Cinema Ltd

$'000s	Jan	Feb	Mar
Cash inflow			
Receipts	22	24	26
Cash outflow			
Payments	27	22	16
Net cash flow	(5)	A	D
Opening balance	2	B	E
Closing balance	(3)	C	F

Appendix 3

Liquidity ratios for The Reel Cinema Ltd

	2015	2016	2017
Current ratio	1.6	1.4	1.2
Acid test ratio	1.1	0.9	0.6

1 a Explain **two** reasons why The Reel Cinema would need to raise finance.

Reason 1:

Explanation:

Reason 2:

Explanation:

[8]

b In order to invest in the latest screening technology, The Reel Cinema is considering **three** options to raise finance:

- retained profit
- leasing
- bank loan.

Which method of finance do you think that The Reel Cinema should choose? Justify your answer.

Retained profit:

Leasing:

Bank loan:

Conclusion:

[12]

2 a Explain **two** reasons why cash-flow forecasting is important to The Reel Cinema.

Reason 1:

Explanation:

Reason 2:

Explanation:

[8]

b Appendix 2 shows The Reel Cinema's net cash flows for the first three months of the coming year.

Complete the net cash-flow statement by putting in figures for A–F. How do you think that The Reel Cinema should deal with the net cash-flow situation in January and February? Justify your answer.

Figures for A–F:

Conclusion:

[12]

3 a Explain why The Reel Cinema's income statement would be useful to the following stakeholders:

- shareholders
- employees
- lenders
- government.

Shareholders:

Employees:

Lenders:

Government:

[8]

b Appendix 1 shows the income statement for The Reel Cinema for the last three years.

Complete the income statement for The Reel Cinema by putting in the figures for A–F. Does the income statement show an improvement in The Reel Cinema's performance? Justify your answer.

Figures for A–F:

Conclusion:

[12]

4 a The stakeholders at The Reel Cinema use the following ratios to analyse the business's performance:

- gross profit margin
- profit margin
- current ratio
- acid test ratio.

Explain what each of these ratios tells you about a business's performance.

Gross profit margin:

Profit margin:

Current ratio:

Acid test ratio:

[8]

b Appendix 3 shows the acid test and current ratios for The Reel Cinema.

What does change in the acid test and current ratios tell you about the change in The Reel Cinema's liquidity over the period? Do you think that the change in liquidity is significant? Justify your answer.

Acid test ratio:

Current ratio:

Conclusion:

[12]

Total available marks: 80

Answering exam-style practice question e

Here is a sample answer to exam-style practice question e. The answer contains some common weaknesses. Read each part and consider how the answer could be improved.

Canvas has seen a fall in profits from 2016 to 2017, which means a fall in performance [App]. One ratio to analyse this is gross profit margin, which is:

gross profit/sales

80/170 = 0.47

70/180 = 0.39

This shows that the gross profit margin has fallen [App], which means that Canvas Ltd is not performing as well. Canvas Ltd could also use the net profit margin, which is:

net profit/sales

20/170 = 0.12

5/180 = 0.027

The net profit margin also shows a fall in performance.

Improve the answer...

There are some ways to improve this answer. Did you think about these?

This answer identifies two relevant ratios to measure Canvas Ltd's performance – gross profit margin and profit margin – although the ratios used are not quite correct because they are not expressed as percentages. The figures have been interpreted correctly as showing a decline in performance.

There is no attempt at evaluation by considering how the non-monetary factor, product quality, could be considered in judging Canvas Ltd's performance. This could have been developed by being more specific about the relationship between product quality and performance.

Answering exam-style case study question 3b

Here is a sample answer to exam-style case study question 3b. The answer contains some common weaknesses. Read each part and consider how the answer could be improved.

Figures for A–F: Here is the completed income statement for The Reel Cinema for 2015, 2016 and 2017.

	2015	2016	2017
Revenue	$210 000	$222 000	$256 000
Cost of sales	$120 000	$135 000	$167 000
Gross profit	$90 000	$87 000	$98 000
Expenses	$62 000	$67 000	$81 000
Profit	$28 000	$20 000	$17 000

Conclusion: The income statement shows that profit over the period has fallen from $28 000 to $17 000 [App] and this would represent a decline in The Reel Cinema's performance [An]. The gross profit, however, has increased from 2015 to 2017 from $90 000 to $98 000. Although gross profit does fall in 2016, there is an overall improvement over the period [Ev]. The revenues over the period have increased, which suggests better performance but costs have also increased [Ev].

Improve the answer...

There are some ways to improve this answer. Did you think about these?

The start is good, with accurate calculations of gross and net profits which are clearly set out in the income statement for The Reel Cinema for 2015, 2016 and 2017. The analysis of the business's performance from the net profit figure is correctly interpreted. The analysis of gross profit is also good with the explanation that gross profits have fallen and then increased with an overall increase over the period. It would have been useful for the answer to consider the reasons for the fall in profit but rise in gross profit by considering how a rise in the business's expenses would have accounted for the different performance figures. The point about revenue showing an improvement in performance but cost control showing a decline is accurate, but the answer could have gone further by focusing on expenses being the main reason for the fall in The Reel Cinema's profit.

Section 6
External influences on business activity

24 Economic issues

Learning summary

Before completing the activities in this unit, you should review your work on the following business topics:

- the economic objectives of any government
- the main stages of the business cycle
- how changes in taxes, government spending and interest rates affect business activity
- how businesses respond to these changes.

KEY TERMS

Gross domestic product (GDP): the value of all goods and services produced by a country in a year.

Inflation: the price increase of goods and services over time.

Exports: the goods and services sold by one country to other countries in return for foreign exchange.

Imports: the goods and services bought by a country from other countries.

Balance of payments: the difference between the value of export and import of goods and services of a country over a year.

Tax: a charge/fee paid to the government on income, goods and services.

Interest rate: the cost to a person or business of borrowing money from a lender such as a bank.

Activity 24.1

This activity will help you to demonstrate your understanding of the economic objectives of a government and how they vary with the different stages of the business cycle.

The **gross domestic product (GDP)** of Qatar has been increasing, there are plenty of jobs in the economy, **inflation** is controlled and the standard of living of the people is rising. The **exports** have been rising and the **imports** have been decreasing consistently for the past two years. The government is very happy with the economic indicators and is confident that it will meet its short-term economic objectives.

a State which stage of the business cycle Qatar's economy is in. **[2]**

b Explain the economic objectives of the government of Qatar and their current status. **[6]**

c Explain **two** economic indicators of Qatar and the impact of their current levels on the consumers and businesses of Qatar. **[6]**

d Explain why a low level of unemployment and a positive **balance of payments** are important objectives for the government of Qatar. **[4]**

Activity 24.2

In this activity, you will have to use your knowledge and understanding of how a government controls its main sources of income and analyse its impact on consumers and businesses.

The government of New Zealand has been reviewing its fiscal policies, with an aim to increase its income so that it can spend more on improved public services. The government has decided to raise the indirect taxes and reduce income **tax** rates.

a State **two** main sources of a government's income. **[2]**

b Identify **two** sources of indirect taxes that New Zealand can raise. **[4]**

Figure 24.1 shows the corporation tax rate over the past four years.

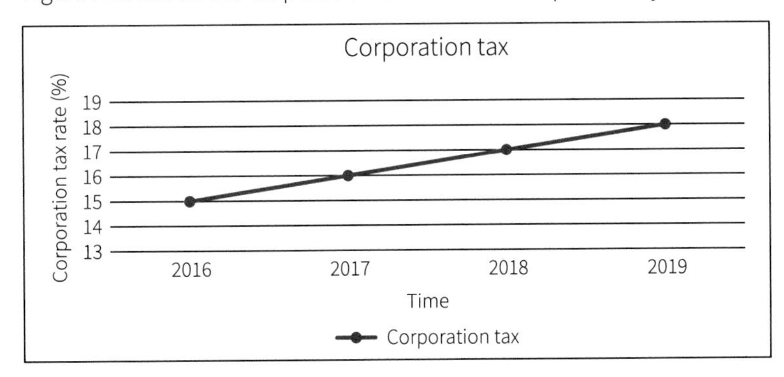

Figure 24.1

c Outline the change in the corporation tax rate over the past four years. **[2]**

First, analyse the graph and identify the change/trend.

Support this with data from the graph.

d Identify **two** effects of the changes in the corporation tax rate on the businesses in New Zealand. **[4]**

e Explain the effect of the decrease in income tax rate on the consumers and businesses in New Zealand. **[4]**

f Do you think that the increase in indirect tax rates and the changes in direct tax rates will increase the income for the government of New Zealand? Justify your answer. **[6]**

Remember, there is no right or wrong answer. Just remember to justify your answer.

TIP

When evaluating a business decision, always consider both the benefits and the shortcomings.

Activity 24.3

In this activity, you will be using your knowledge and understanding of how governments control the amount of money in circulation by changing interest rates.

ABC Bicycles manufactures bicycles in the United States and is thinking of expanding its operations. Table 24.1 shows the interest rates in the last four years. ABC's finance manager is worried about the impact of increasing interest rates on the costs. He has also just been informed that the corporation tax rate has been decreased by the government.

Year	Interest rate (%)
2016	2
2017	2.5
2018	2.8
2019	3.0

Table 24.1

a Define '**interest rate**'? **[2]**

b Calculate the amount of interest that will have to be paid in the year 2019 on an amount of $500 000. **[2]**

c Explain the effect of increasing interest rates on the consumers of the United States. **[4]**

d Explain the effect of increasing interest rates on ABC Bicycles. **[4]**

Try to answer the question in context by using information from the question.

e Do you think that the finance manager of ABC Bicycles should be worried about the increasing interest rates and decrease in corporation tax rate? **[6]**

Remember to use information from the context.

Reflection: What skills do you think were useful in answering the data-based questions?

25 Environmental and ethical issues

Learning summary

Before completing the activities in this unit, you should review your work on the following business topics:

- the impact of business activity on the environment
- the external costs and benefits of business decisions
- sustainable development
- environmental pressures and opportunities
- ethical issues faced by businesses.

KEY TERMS

Sustainable development: a business activity is said to be sustainable if it has a positive overall impact on the environment and its stakeholders, ensuring its survival in the future.

Cost–benefit analysis: analysis of the costs and benefits of a project, the focus being on the social costs and benefits.

Externality: the effect of business activities on unrelated parties.

Social benefit: the positive impact of a business decision on society.

Social cost: the negative impact of a business decision on society.

Activity 25.1

This activity will check your understanding of the impact of business activity on the environment and society.

Synta Plastics plans to set up a new manufacturing plant near a major city. It plans to manufacture household items made out of recycled plastic. It has presented its proposal but is waiting for the government's approval. The government has recently introduced very tough environmental regulations. In its proposal, Synta Plastics has included a plan for proper waste disposal from its factory and **sustainable development**. It has published a statement saying that it has conducted a **cost–benefit analysis** and that its negative externalities will be minimal compared to the benefits.

a Define 'externalities'. **[2]**

b Identify **one** positive and **one** negative **externality** that may be caused by Synta Plastics. **[4]**

Examples may be useful in identifying the points.

c Outline **two** steps that Synta Plastics can take to be sustainable. **[4]**

d Do you think that Synta Plastics will have greater **social benefits** than **social costs**? Justify your answer. **[6]**

Activity 25.2

In this activity, you will have to use your knowledge and understanding of how pressure groups work and how businesses respond to environmental pressures.

Tastybites is an international fast-food chain serving food from all over the world. It wants to expand by starting operations in a new country. Tastybites hopes to benefit from the low cost of labour and gain access to more consumers.

However, there has been a lot of negative press about this venture in the country it has chosen and pressure groups are filing a petition to oppose this. They are holding demonstrations saying that it will be bad for the environment because of the amount of packaging and waste produced by disposable ware. They also claim that Tastybites will be harmful for health and will hurt the small restaurant/fast-food businesses in the country. The pressure groups are lobbying to persuade the government to revisit its legal controls.

a Define 'pressure group'. **[2]**

b Identify **three** methods used by the pressure groups to make their point. **[4]**

c Consider why it is important for Tastybites to respond to the threats and opportunities posed by the pressure groups. **[4]**

Remember to answer the question in context as Tastybites hasn't started operations yet.

d Do you think that the government can use legal controls to minimise the negative effects of business activity by businesses such as Tastybites? Justify your answer. **[6]**

Look at both aspects of legal controls (restrictive measures as well as incentives) in order to fully evaluate their impact.

TIP

When evaluating a business decision, always develop the knowledge points/factors and analyse them fully instead of listing various factors. This analysis will help you come to a well-justified evaluation.

Activity 25.3

This activity relies on your understanding of ethical issues faced by businesses and the conflict that they have between profits and ethics when making business decisions.

Techno Ltd manufactures low-cost electronic devices and is beginning to sell its products in the international market. It has been facing a lot of opposition from pressure groups worldwide due to its suspected unethical business practices. Pressure groups claim that workers at Techno Ltd have dangerous working conditions, unreasonable workloads and have long working hours without the appropriate compensation. Recently, there was an article published about the lack of sufficient health and safety measures from the toxic vapours produced in its factories.

Techno Ltd denies the claims but, due to mounting pressure from pressure groups and the government, it is reviewing its business practices in order to make them more ethical.

a Define 'ethical business practices'. **[2]**

b Explain **two** unethical business practices of Techno Ltd claimed by the pressure groups. **[4]**

Read the information in the question carefully to identify the claims made by the pressure groups about Techno Ltd's unethical business practices and explain the impact on the workers.

c Do you think that Techno Ltd should invest in making its business practices more ethical? Justify your answer. **[6]**

TIP

In questions requiring the skills of analysis, application and evaluation, choosing the right knowledge points/factors to develop further is very important. Choose the knowledge points that can be analysed in detail, support multiple points of view and relate well to the business in context.

Reflection: Are you now better able to apply your answers to the given scenario? Why do you think that this is the case?

26 Business and the international economy

Learning summary

Before completing the activities in this unit, you should review your work on the following business topics:

- globalisation
- multinational companies
- exchange rate changes.

KEY TERMS

Globalisation: the process by which countries are connected with each other because of the trade of goods and services.

Multinational company: an organisation that has operations in more than one country.

Exchange rate: the rate at which one country's currency can be exchanged for that of another.

Host country: the foreign country where a multinational sets up its operations.

Appreciation: a currency is said to appreciate if the value of the currency increases with respect to another currency.

Activity 26.1

This activity checks your knowledge and understanding of key concepts and also requires you to analyse the impact of multinational companies and apply this to the given scenario.

Moto Automobiles is a successful automobile manufacturer based in Switzerland. It exports its cars and trucks to various countries in the region. The senior executives of the company think that it should take advantage of **globalisation**. It is considering setting up a manufacturing plant in Singapore and becoming a **multinational company**.

a Define the term 'globalisation'. **[2]**

b Explain **two** reasons why Moto Automobiles may want to become a multinational company. **[6]**

Break this down into stages so that you are demonstrating each skill in turn.

Think of two benefits.

Try to use some of the terms and information given in the question.

Explain the effect of the benefits you have mentioned on Moto Automobiles.

TIP
Remember that there is no right or wrong answer but do support your opinion with reasons.

c Would Singapore benefit from allowing Moto Automobiles to begin operations there? Justify your answer. **[6]**

Try to think of both an advantage and a disadvantage to Singapore.

Activity 26.2

This activity checks your understanding of the factors to be considered by companies when doing business internationally.

Tinsel Toys makes toys and video games and has a factory in India. With an aim to grow its business, it started exporting its toys to its neighbouring country, Pakistan, five years ago. Pakistan has a good potential market and sales have been increasing every year.

In the last year, however, the profits have decreased considerably. The directors think that this is due to new tariffs and quotas imposed by Pakistan. Tinsel Toys is evaluating whether setting up operations in Pakistan and becoming a multinational may be a more profitable option than just exporting to Pakistan.

a Define the term 'tariff'. **[2]**

b Outline the possible effects of tariffs and quotas on Tinsel Toys. **[4]**

c Explain **two** factors that Tinsel Toys should consider before setting up operations in Pakistan. **[6]**

Activity 26.3

This activity relies on your understanding of exchange rates. The last question tests your ability to analyse the impact of exchange rate changes on importers and exporters and your ability to develop a link to the impact on consumers.

Baby Needs is an established company producing baby products in China. It sells its products to many countries in the region that are part of a trade bloc, though it mainly exports its products to the United States. The exchange rate between China's currency (CH) and the United States's currency (US) is:

CH:US is 1:3

a State how being part of a trade bloc could be beneficial to Baby Needs. **[2]**

b Calculate the value of 20 000 CH in the United States's currency. **[2]**

Use your knowledge of what exchange rate means. If you're not sure about this, check Unit 26 'Business and the international economy' in your coursebook to make sure that you understand it.
The value of China's currency appreciates against the value of the United States's currency.

c Define the term '**appreciation**'. **[2]**

Remember that appreciation should be considered with respect to another currency, in this case US.

d Explain the effect of the appreciation of currency CH against currency US on Baby Needs and the consumers in the United States. **[6]**

TIP
When explaining or analysing, make sure that you have considered cost and/or revenue – it's not enough to simply state that there might be an increase in profits.

Reflection: Think about which questions you find difficult. Why were they difficult? Was it a gap in your knowledge and understanding or did you find it difficult to structure your answer?

Exam-style practice questions

All exam-style practice questions and sample answers in this title were written by the author(s). In examinations, the way marks are awarded may be different.

Universal Stores is a department store that sells stylish homeware, home appliances, high-quality food and fashion. It has an international customer base and has stores in five neighbouring countries. It recognises the importance of globalisation and wants to open up stores in two new countries. The first country's economy is in the growth stages and the second country has very low taxes.

The management team of Universal Stores is confident that it will do well in both countries because it has ethical and sustainable business practices, but it is aware that it needs to consider the different cultures and the political uncertainty in these countries as well.

a Define the term 'multinational company'. **[2]**

b Define 'sustainable development'. **[2]**

c State **four** benefits to Universal Stores of being a multinational company. **[4]**

d Explain **two** ways that a company like Universal Stores can be ethical. **[6]**

e Do you think that its ethical and sustainable business practices alone will ensure Universal Stores's success in the new countries? Should it be worried about their different cultures and the political uncertainty there? Justify your answer. **[6]**

Total available marks: 20

Exam-style case study

Foo Desserts

The last five years have been good for Foo Desserts. The business was set up by Mateo and Valeria, who left leading management positions with a multinational food manufacturer to start it. The business specialises in high-priced, luxury desserts targeted at high-income consumers. The business is based in Mexico and has benefitted from strong economic growth in the Mexican economy, as shown in Appendix 1.

A new government has, however, increased income tax and tax on company profits to fund increased government expenditure on health and education and this has made trading conditions more difficult for Foo Desserts. Mexico's central bank is thinking about reducing interest rates to keep economic growth going. Mexico's corporation tax is shown in Appendix 2.

The Mexican government is introducing new environmental regulations as it tries to adopt more sustainable development in Mexico. The new policies are being introduced in the next few years and will have consequences for manufacturing businesses such as Foo Desserts. Mateo and Valeria see this as an opportunity for their business. They have tried to run Foo Desserts as an ethical business and achieving ethical objectives is seen as key to the organisation's direction.

Mateo and Valeria want to turn Foo Desserts into a multinational company by opening plants in Brazil and Argentina. They want to take the opportunities and benefits that come from globalisation as they try to grow their business.

Appendix 1

Mexico's economic growth

2013	2014	2015	2016	2017
2.1%	2.3%	2.2%	2.8%	3.2%

Appendix 2

Mexico's corporation tax

2016	2017
19%	26%

Appendix 3

Mexico's Income tax

2016	2017
24%	26%

1 **a** Using the data in Appendix 1, explain **one** possible advantage and **one** disadvantage for Foo Desserts from Mexican economic growth.

Advantage:

Explanation:

Disadvantage:

Explanation:

[8]

b Using the data in Appendices 2 and 3, explain why the following **three** factors resulting from a rise in taxation are disadvantages to Foo Desserts:

- Consumers have less income.
- Employees might not be as motivated.
- The business has less funding for investment.

Which disadvantage is the most important? Justify your answer.

Consumers have less income:

Employees might not be as motivated:

The business has less funding for investment:

Conclusion:

[12]

2 **a** Explain **two** benefits to Foo Desserts of a cut in interest rates.

Benefit 1:

Explanation:

Benefit 2:

Explanation:

[8]

b Explain how the following factors might be affected by the Mexican government's new environmental regulations:

- business costs
- administration and bureaucracy
- relationships with the local community.

Which effects do you think would have the **most** important impact on Foo Desserts? Justify your answer.

Business costs:
Administration and bureaucracy:
Relationships with the local community:
Conclusion:

[12]

3 a Explain **four** ways that Foo Desserts might be affected by the government's focus on more sustainable development in Mexico.

Way 1:
Explanation:

Way 2:
Explanation:

Way 3:
Explanation:

Way 4:
Explanation:

[8]

b Explain how the following **three** factors might be affected by a more ethical approach by Foo Desserts:

- brand image and reputation
- motivation of employees
- increased cost of materials.

Which do you think is the **most** important factor affecting Foo Desserts? Justify your answer.

Brand image and reputation:
Motivation of employees:
Increased cost of materials:
Conclusion:

[12]

4 a Explain **four** benefits of globalisation for Foo Desserts.

Benefit 1:
Explanation:

Benefit 2:
Explanation:

Benefit 3:
Explanation:

Benefit 4:

Explanation:

[8]

b Foo Desserts wants to expand production into other South American countries. Explain **two** advantages and **two** disadvantages of doing this. Do you think that Foo Desserts should become a multinational? Justify your answer.

Advantage 1:

Advantage 2:

Disadvantage 1:

Disadvantage 2:

Conclusion:

[12]

Total available marks: 80

Answering exam-style practice question d

Here is a sample answer to exam-style practice question d. The answer contains some common weaknesses. Read each part and consider how the answer could be improved.

Way 1: Fair treatment of all employees [K].

Explanation: Though Universal Stores has stores in five different countries [App], it must treat all workers fairly irrespective of the country that they are operating in.

Way 2: Source the goods that it sells from ethical suppliers [K].

Explanation: Universal Stores should make sure that the people who make its products are not being exploited or have unsafe working conditions [An].

Improve the answer...

There are some ways to improve this answer. Did you think about these?

Way 1: Fair treatment of all employees is a way of being ethical and the answer shows good application by mentioning ‘five different countries’. However, it hasn’t really explained how a business can treat employees fairly.

Way 2: The answer makes a valid point and is explained well. It is just missing application to the business in context.

Answering exam-style case study 1b

Here is a sample answer to exam-style case study 1b. The answer contains some common weaknesses. Read each part and consider how the answer could be improved.

Consumers have less income: As income taxation increases, the consumers who buy Foo Desserts' products may have less income [K] which could lead to a fall in their spending on the goods they buy [App]. This may mean that Foo Desserts' customers spend less on desserts, which leads to a fall in the business's revenues and profits [An]. This will, however, depend on how responsive Foo's products are to a fall in consumer income brought about by the rise in taxation [Ev].

Employees might not be as motivated: A rise in income tax could mean that employees at Foo take home less pay [App] because of higher tax, which could reduce motivation at work [An]. The extent to which this affects their motivation may depend on the size of the tax increase [Ev]. If it is significant, then this could reduce their motivation at work and have a big effect on productivity at Foo [Ev].

The business has less funding for investment: Higher tax on profits, as shown in Appendix 2, may reduce the funds that Foo has for investment in capital and innovation [App]. If the company has less money for new machinery and equipment, it may be forced to borrow or cancel investment projects [An]. The extent to which this is true will depend on whether the profits tax affects Foo and the other sources of finance that it has access to [Ev].

Conclusion: The most significant disadvantage of the tax increase is the impact that it has on investment. Consumers' spending on desserts is probably quite low so a tax on their income will not have much effect [Ev]. Tax on employees may not affect worker motivation because of the number of other factors affecting motivation [Ev]. The tax on profits, however, has a very direct effect on the funds for investment [Ev].

Improve the answer...

There are some ways to improve this answer. Did you think about these?

The first point made about consumer income is clearly explained and applied. There is some effective application in terms of Foo's revenue and profits, but this could be developed further by considering the luxury nature of the product and how this might be affected by a fall in consumer income. The answer goes on to consider how a tax rise might affect worker motivation and this is quite well applied in terms of Foo's productivity. There is some evaluation, although there could have been some consideration of the nature of Foo's workforce and how their motivation is affected by money. The next section deals with the impact of tax on investment. There is reference to Appendix 2, but this could be developed to show the significance of the increase in taxation. The answer is, however, clearly applied to Foo by considering the impact on investment projects. This is evaluated by considering other sources of finance. The final conclusion effectively focuses on the tax on profits as the most important disadvantage.